LEADING
REMOTELY

Achieving success in a
globally connected world

LEADING
REMOTELY

MIKE PARKES

BLOOMSBURY BUSINESS
LONDON • OXFORD • NEW YORK • NEW DELHI • SYDNEY

BLOOMSBURY BUSINESS
Bloomsbury Publishing Plc
50 Bedford Square, London, WC1B 3DP, UK
29 Earlsfort Terrace, Dublin 2, Ireland

First published in Great Britain 2021

For legal purposes the Acknowledgements on p.ix
constitute an extension of this copyright page

A catalogue record for this book is available from the British Library

Library of Congress Cataloguing-in-Publication data has been applied for

ISBN: 978-1-4729-9119-5; eBook: 978-1-4729-9118-8

2 4 6 8 10 9 7 5 3 1

Typeset by Deanta Global Publishing Services, Chennai, India
Printed and bound in Great Britain by CPI Group (UK) Ltd, Croydon CR0 4YY

To find out more about our authors and books visit www.bloomsbury.com
and sign up for our newsletters

About the author

Mike Parkes, Chartered MCIPD

Mike has worked with managers, executives and directors for over 35 years, guiding and advising them with their leadership challenges. His first book *Business Facilitation: an essential leadership skill for employee engagement* was published in March 2014. He has been the designer and lead facilitator, for over 15 years, of the British Retail Consortium's Retail Masters at the Saïd Business School, University of Oxford.

Mike was one of the founding directors of Momentum Development Ltd in 2001, now Momentum Results LLP, and before that he was CEO of The Development Associates Group Ltd, a subsidiary of the global accountancy firm Deloitte. He joined as a senior consultant in 1987, before progressing to managing consultant and CEO in 1997. Prior to this he worked for The Prudential, Luton Airport and Tesco.

Mike is renowned for his practical, insightful, and commercial approach and over the years has spoken at leadership conferences across the globe in the US, Asia, Australasia, the Middle East, South Africa and throughout Europe. In 2020, he spoke at over 100 virtual leadership events on 'Leading Remotely' and 'Managing Performance in the Virtual World'.

www.momentumresults.net

Contents

Acknowledgements

The foundation for this book started over 15 years ago when the initial research began. I would like to thank my former colleagues and long-term friends, Andy Norton and Sue Kluss, for all their input and experiences in the formative years. More recently, I'd also like to thank Derek Linden for his ongoing contribution, particularly during the pandemic period.

Above all, I'd like to thank all the highly respected leaders who I've listed below, who I have known for so many years and have provided so much insight, experience and value to the richness of this book.

Martyn Brett-Lee: Commercial Director, Welcome Break

Shona Cronley: Global Director of Talent & Engagement, Hotelbeds Group

Stuart Dale: Chief Commercial Officer, Bakuun.com

Debbie Edwards: Vice President and General Manager Europe, Gap

Vanessa Evans: Global HR Director, Rentokil Initial

Steve Finlan: Chief Executive Officer, The Wine Society

Jon France: General Manager Operations and Property Australia, Big W

Mike Hawes: Senior Vice President, HR International, Avis Budget Group

Ian Herrett: former Chief Executive Officer, Bathstore

Patrick McGillycuddy: Sales Director, Volkswagen Group UK

Gill Palfrey-Hill: UK Global Talent and OE Director, Costa Coffee (formerly Director of Global Talent & Development, Specsavers)

Anil Patel: Chairman, Virtual Manager

Ravindra (Ravi) Patel: former Managing Director, Middle East and Eastern Europe, Kodak

Jeremy Phillips-Powell: Group Talent Director, Rentokil Initial

Sohail Shaikh: Chief Executive Officer Global Franchise, Hamleys

Michelle Wald: US Country Manager, Tony's Chocolonely

Richard Walgate: Director, North Division, B&Q

Penny Weatherup: Human Resources Director, Volkswagen Group UK

Axel Zeltner: Director, Deloitte Deutschland

Finally, I'd like to thank my wife, Alison, for her support, as well as compiling, editing and producing this book.

Foreword

I've always been brought up to value the importance of evidence-based research. As an academic, while some of my colleagues enjoy concepts and theories, I'm never happier than when looking for patterns and trends in the real world and matching them with how I think the world might work. In the area of leadership, it has to be said that we are not short of theory. Most airport lounge (or, these days, coffee table) books are still offering would-be leaders '10 Steps to Heaven' based on scant first-hand evidence. And so it is enormously refreshing to read a timely collection of practical insights and recommendations on leading remotely – based not just on the more than 30 years' experience that Mike Parkes brings to the understanding of leadership itself, but also the evidence drawn from highly respected leaders in action, from a diverse range of sectors.

There's a particular need for such insight at the moment. We need different kinds of leadership during the present health, economic and social crises. As we hear from the range of acknowledged leaders interviewed for this book, supported by the research evidence, leading remotely is not about 'centralized control' – a culture still very common in large organizations with high-profile personalities creating dependency. The most effective leaders today are more likely to have the attributes of what has been termed a 'post-heroic' style. Such an approach stresses qualities that include empowerment, collaborative decision-making, ownership and a willingness to engender imaginative solutions and ideas from talent and teams throughout the organization.

Professor Jonathan Reynolds,
Saïd Business School, University of Oxford

CHAPTER ONE

Leading Remotely – The Fundamental Questions

Introduction

In 2006, Anil Patel was the regional operations manager for over 300 Royal Dutch Shell plc sites in Australia, covering New South Wales, Victoria and Tasmania, having previously worked as a consultant for Accenture plc, the global professional services company, in Switzerland, the Netherlands, Hong Kong and Australia. Anil has an incisive and sharp mind, grasps concepts quickly and has a real ability to see through difficult and complex situations, but nothing would prepare him to lead remotely as this role did.

With so many sites over such a diverse region and responsibilities for retail, merchandising and operations, Anil was stretched. Over the next three years he worked tirelessly, tenaciously and at pace, achieving great results despite the fact, because of the remote nature of his role, he was often the last to hear about problems and issues. In fact, he'd often only be aware of the situation once it had grown in magnitude and was being raised by a major brand/ supplier who was experiencing difficulties across a number of his sites. Driven by this, Anil created a groundbreaking approach (this is described in further detail in Chapter 5).

In many ways, this epitomizes one of the key challenges for the remote or multi-site leader: how do you stay close to the business while operating from afar? This book not only addresses this challenge but also the conundrums of:

- How does the remote leader achieve results from afar without micromanaging?
- How does the remote leader galvanize everyone in their team behind a common direction without being everywhere at once?
- Which decisions does the remote leader handle themselves and which do they let go?
- How do they encourage others to take responsibility, while still retaining accountability?
- How does the remote leader add real value rather than merely creating disruption?
- How do they move the business forward without doing it all themselves?
- What fundamental elements distinguish an outstanding remote leader from average or poor leaders?

This book examines the skills and leadership challenges of today's leaders who are remotely leading teams on different sites, in different countries and even different continents. Following the coronavirus pandemic, remote leadership transitioned from being a skill synonymous with those in regional or divisional roles in organizations to becoming a fundamental skill for every leader as more and more individuals and teams work remotely. The book shares 15 years of empirical research into what makes remote leadership effective. This has been established by assessing leaders' results and observing them in action, corroborated with data and insights from their colleagues, teams and their own leaders, all cross-referenced to business metrics and performance. This research has been undertaken widely in various industries, including the retail, travel, insurance, banking and automotive sectors.

The book also features the remote leadership experiences, insights and practical tips of 10 highly respected senior leaders in widely recognized businesses across the globe and describes how they have succeeded in this complex and challenging area of leadership. Finally, the book features the recent challenges of leading individuals and teams through the coronavirus pandemic and provides a wealth of practical insight from high-achieving remote leaders, in a wide range of sectors, on what they actually did.

Context

For over 20 years, leadership development company Momentum Results LLP has worked with leaders at all levels of business, helping them develop their leadership capability and succeed in navigating the day-to-day and emerging challenges of their roles, as well as helping many transition to more senior roles. This transitioning has included:

First Line Managers	→	Middle Managers
Middle Managers	→	Senior Managers
Senior Managers	→	Divisional Roles
Divisional Roles	→	Directors
Directors	→	Executive/Main Board

These transitions each have their own unique challenges. However, despite the increasing accountability as individuals have progressed up the hierarchy, our years of experience have shown that **the toughest transition occurs when leaders make**

their first step out of a single-site location and move to multi-site responsibility or when their teams are no longer located in one fixed site.

Our work in this field has enabled us to gain invaluable insights, experience and learning that have helped leaders to not only transition into the role, but also for the more experienced remote leaders to excel in the role. That said, our experience has shown that many highly experienced leaders in single-site locations have struggled in their transition to remote leadership.

> Why do highly successful single-site leaders often struggle to make the transition to multi-site/leading remotely?

Past success isn't necessarily an indicator of future success

The most highly rated single-site leaders usually attain this status, understandably, due to the results they have achieved in terms of sales, profitability, management of the cost base, employee engagement and customer satisfaction, as well as how they manage their relationships upwards. Though these indicators are undoubtedly essential, they give no insight into how the leader achieves these results.

In the early days of our work with leaders, we were often introduced to individuals who were deemed to have potential to step up into a remote leadership role – in fact, for many, they were next in line. Their results stood out from their colleagues', they managed visits well and built strong, trustworthy relationships with those above; however, behind the scenes, their achievements did not always provide a firm foundation for future success. We could clearly see that the way they led in a single site would not easily enable them to lead multi-sites or remote teams.

Example 1

In this first example, Marc worked for a large retailer, had extensive experience and his team had huge respect for him, both professionally and personally. They recognized his knowledge and his skill and, as a result, tended to rely upon him. The team would look to him for direction and he was only too keen to share his ideas, thinking and above all, his decisions. Issues that arose in his absence were saved up for discussion on his return – in effect, creating a level of dependency upon him.

Marc did not have an autocratic, commanding or domineering style, far from it; however, he did tend to take on too much himself and his team readily passed decisions, issues and problems upwards. This wasn't because of any lack of commitment on their part, but fear of getting it wrong and letting him down. As a consequence, his business results were good but largely at the detriment of his own health and well-being as he found himself under constant pressure from the excessive involvement and workload he took on. Fundamentally, his eagerness to help meant that he stepped in too early, took on too much responsibility himself and failed to create ownership in his teams to take decisions themselves.

Example 2

In this second example in a telecoms company, Claire was very charismatic, highly respected but very controlling. Her results were excellent, largely because she placed herself at the centre of everything. Very little happened without her agreement and in fact, she was very much the initiator of everything that was new. She provided detailed plans, briefings and direction for all team members, who were highly committed and dedicated. However, the level of control she exerted meant that everything was passed to or had to go through her and as a result, created a different form of dependency to that described in Example 1.

Once more though her results were excellent; this was largely achieved through her own efforts and over-reliance on her own decision-making, which is a difficult strategy to sustain when leading a range of teams remotely. With this approach in the remote leadership role, short of charging around trying to do everything they did before, but in several locations all at once, the reality is that they are more absent than present and therefore unable to constantly step in and make decisions for the teams.

In response to this, buoyed by the view that their style and ways of operating have served them well in the past, there can be a tendency for leaders who adopt this approach to retain control through the application of rigid processes and procedures. Depending upon the number and frequency of their use, this tends to dilute the onsite team's ability to think, act and make the right decisions themselves.

> Why do the skills that served single-site leaders well become less effective in remote leadership roles?

Engendering ownership and responsibility

Leaders succeed because of the decisions they make and the ways in which these decisions are reached. With remote leadership, leaders are inevitably far more removed from the action, as the 'remote' title suggests, and as a result, they need to make different types of decisions.

- Could others on site take that decision?
- How could I support without taking responsibility away from the team?
- How can I help them become more effective at making the right decisions in ways that they become self-standing?
- To what extent are issues being stored up for when I am around?

In many ways, remote leaders succeed through the decisions they *don't* take themselves! Instead, leading remotely requires clarity of direction and greater ownership and responsibility taken by those closest to the problem.

The traditional dilemma for leaders on single sites is that they are rarely ever more than one day away from addressing, resolving and rectifying any problems. They can step in, make decisions and head off problems with relative ease. In contrast, remote leaders might not even be aware of issues for some significant period of time despite the quality of communication channels. Equally, not every decision or issue can be delayed or deferred to those above. The ability to engender ownership, commitment and responsibility is fundamental to the success of the remote leader. However, many single-site leaders achieve great results without this ability, doing so through their own determination, resilience and decision-making. Unfortunately for some, this only becomes transparent once they step into the remote leadership role. Only then do they recognize the need to adapt their style and develop a new skill set, which often proves incredibly challenging in terms of changing their behaviours and habits learned in a business lifetime.

Being inquisitive and diagnostic

Some single-site leaders are naturally inquisitive; they succeed because they are curious in unlocking information from others, even if they believe that they have a full understanding of a situation. They view understanding how others perceive a situation, and their mindset around this, as fundamental to unlocking any problem. This inquisitive and diagnostic approach, rather than a directive or interrogative approach, which may have an underlying accusatory nature such as 'Why have you done that?', 'What were you thinking?', enables the leader to understand what is happening and more importantly, the thinking underpinning this from afar. This understanding results in the leader unlocking the real cause of a problem rather than the apparent causes, which tend to be symptoms. Unfortunately for many single-site leaders, they are so close to the action that they believe they:

- know the context;
- know the challenges;
- know the causes;
- know the issues.

Therefore, they believe that they know the solutions. As a result, they tend to guide, advise and advocate based on their knowledge, what they have done in the past and above all, what has become second nature to them. These leaders, in particular, find it hard to transition into a remote leadership role as they lack the core inquisition and curiosity skills to diagnose issues from afar.

In the new data-rich world, this can often be intensified as leaders are provided with detailed analysis of everything that happens. As a result, the remote leader also:

- knows the context;
- knows the challenges;
- knows the causes;
- knows the issues.

They may enter into dialogue with preconceived ideas and views rather than using the data to encourage a joint dialogue with natural exploration of the issues to reach the core of a problem and therefore the appropriate solution.

By adopting a more inquisitive and diagnostic approach, leaders unearth the root causes of problems and issues, as well as unlocking individuals' own ability to generate solutions themselves.

Influencing rather than directing

In a single-site leadership role, leaders tend to be naturally absorbed and focused on running their part of the business, ensuring that all individuals and teams are clear on what is expected, deliver on commitments and the operation runs like a smoothly oiled machine. For many, they barely look outside of their part of the business, and if they do, they tend to seek opportunities to reinforce existing thinking; they are, in effect, very insular.

However, step away from that role, into the next level as the remote leader of a number of individuals and teams at numerous locations, and they become involved with a wider span of stakeholders, from colleagues leading other remote locations and key players in central functions to other senior leaders in addition to their direct line leader. This requires a different and more refined skill set of influencing, which involves achieving through others without any power or authority over them. Typically, we have observed many single-site leaders adopting a very empowering and involving style with their teams. However, there is nevertheless a clear line of responsibility and accountability and despite their style, there is a tacit or, for some, explicit understanding that they are the boss. With remote leadership though, that line still exists for direct reports, but the number of stakeholders whom they have to interface with and influence dramatically increases. Many have not sufficiently developed their skill set to influence rather than manage others with different priorities, expectations and needs, which requires tact, diplomacy, clarity and determination.

Prioritizing and leading themselves

Finally, those stepping into a remote leadership role often suddenly find their working day is dramatically different from leading in a single-site context. The remote leader can feel very isolated, often spending significant amounts of time on their own, travelling to the various locations by car, plane or having touch points virtually. Clearly, with the onset of the radical changes induced by the coronavirus pandemic, this is likely to result in long-term changes and this is discussed directly in Chapter 5.

The nature of the remote leader role means that no longer are they embroiled in the day-to-day operations of the sites where often their day passes in the blink of an eye. Now they have to stand back, consider where to become involved and prioritize their time and energy:

- to ensure that time is not wasted and consumed in getting from one location to another;
- to determine where they focus their attention;

- to decide who, when and how they interact with individuals and teams from afar;
- to evaluate how they add value rather than interfere and become an unnecessary distraction.

Some remote leaders struggle with the potentially solitary nature of the role, missing the excitement, stimulation and constant challenges of a single site.

> Why do new remote leaders often find the transition and new challenges initially less rewarding?

What they enjoyed doing in the past as a single-site leader isn't necessarily a key component of the remote leadership role

Single sites, by their very nature, have communities of daily interaction, whether that is with colleagues, customers or suppliers, and these in themselves create daily dialogue, stimulation and engagement. Many single-site leaders thrive on the wear and tear, the rough and tumble of the daily interactions and enjoy being involved in the discussions, debates and above all, the decisions. Single-site leaders therefore become highly skilled in managing these types of interactions and for many they provide a high level of stimulation. Stepping away from this as a remote leader can often leave a vacuum in their working life, so not only is this a void for them, but when they do enter sites, many fall back on the skills and behaviours that served them well in the past. They become embroiled in discussions and debates that they enjoyed in the past, rather than operating at a higher level, bringing broader value and insight and leaving these types of discussions to those who are responsible for the delivery. Fundamentally, what they enjoyed doing in the past, and were probably very good at, is no longer their responsibility.

Finally, there is the fundamental issue that some remote leaders fail to recognize that their behaviour and skills in the new role need to be significantly different but unfortunately, they tend to rely on those that they are most adept and comfortable with. Essentially, they have the misplaced belief that the new role, though having wider responsibilities, is more of the same and doesn't require different attitudes, outlooks, skills and behaviours. As a result, they find themselves battling with the role rather than blossoming within it.

> Why do businesses fail to recognize the skills challenge and therefore don't provide development support for the new remote leader?

The new remote leader has inevitably been successful in a previous role and although they are taking on wider responsibilities and accountabilities, little thought or even tolerance is given to the fact that the new role requires a new skill set. Though their line leader usually recognizes that there won't always be a smooth transition as they adjust to the new role, few others tend to meaningfully recognize this or even realize the new learning required. Equally, the remote leader themselves, having been highly successful in the previous role, has rarely been used to asking for help, support and guidance and therefore has the misplaced belief that in so doing, they are demonstrating a level of weakness or even raising doubts about the decision to appoint them in the first place.

So far, we have discussed why it can be so challenging to transition from single-site to multi-site/remote leadership. In fact, from our experiences, it is the most challenging transition any leader makes. Many are surprised by this statement, as it is assumed that a rise to the very top of an organization is the most challenging, with its attendant range of wider responsibilities and accountabilities such as corporate governance, managing stakeholders, investors and dealing with external bodies. Though new knowledge sets are required, the fundamental skills that provide the foundation for these more senior roles first become a prerequisite and necessity in the multi-site/remote leadership role when an individual steps out from the single-site and begins to lead from afar

In the next chapter, we explore what it takes to be a really successful remote leader and how this differs from those who are average or poor performers.

CHAPTER TWO

The Dilemmas and Behaviours Differentiating the Outstanding from the Average from the Poorer Remote Leader

Between 2005 and 2020, Momentum Results LLP worked with vast numbers of leaders in remote leadership roles, ranging from area managers, regional managers and divisional directors through to country directors, regional directors and those who have global leadership responsibilities.

Over these 15 years and beyond, we have not only worked directly, developing the skills of several hundreds of remote leaders and undertaking empirical research, but we have also observed and analysed many more from afar. Through our work, we have been able to identify from their business results, together with assessments from those above and below, those who were high performers, those who were average performers and those who were poorer performers. From this data, we were able to identify eight dimensions together with the underpinning behaviours. In the last 10 years, we have used this data to develop the skills and expertise of remote leaders across the globe and through the changing nature of the business world have been able to refine the research.

During 2020, with the onset of the coronavirus crisis, social distancing and more extensive use of virtual working were introduced.

These dimensions and supporting behaviours have thus proven even more valid, as verified by hundreds of leaders working remotely, during our virtual global learning sessions and the highly respected leaders whose stories you'll learn of later in this book.

The research

The research didn't start out as a theoretical project. Momentum Results LLP was widely known for its ability to develop the skills and capabilities of leaders, and it was on this basis that we were commissioned to help two high-potential leaders to transition from store managers into regional managers, within a well-known clothing retailer.

At that stage, the retailer had recognized that the success rates of high-performing store managers transitioning into regional roles and continuing to perform well was low. The retailer believed that with our support, the success rate could be increased. With that as a context, before embarking upon any form of development, we were curious as to why seemingly high performers in store roles were less successful in multi-site, regional roles.

We began by working with the existing regional manager (RM) population and on the pretext of helping the new RMs succeed began to obtain insights and data from them. This involved:

1) Diagnostic conversations with each RM on how they viewed the role, the challenges and the skills;
2) Observation of the RMs in the workplace;
3) Informal conversations with team members to calibrate the data from stages 1) and 2);
4) Diagnostic conversations with peers, colleagues in their functions and their line directors.

Although the conversations were very fruitful, the real richness of the data emerged through shadowing RMs in the workplace as they undertook their daily and weekly rituals and interactions with a wide range of stakeholders.

Underpinning this diagnostic process, we cross-referenced all the data to business results. By obtaining the business performance metrics, we were able to establish which RMs, by their results, were performing more successfully than their colleagues. We then compared the behavioural data that we were gathering with the business results and started to group the behaviours under themes.

At the same time, and quite fortuitously, another client engaged with us around the same business issue and we were able to grow the sample size to 36 multi-site leaders. Though statistically not significant at this stage, it nevertheless provided us with nuances that enabled us to test and corroborate the behaviours.

On reflection, I attribute the success of the research to the clients' trust in our understanding of and ability to develop leaders, the fortunate timing of the second group to allow our sample to grow and our determination to really examine what makes the transition effective, using our expertise in being able to observe, identify, define and, most importantly, to describe behaviour.

We regard behaviour as objective, unemotive, factual statements of actions. In contrast, judgements are subjective and emotive; for example:

Judgement: 'He has a negative attitude and is a blocker.'
Behaviour: 'Each time a suggestion was made, he stated why it wouldn't work, rather than how it needed to change and talked over others, pointing out flaws in their argument rather than exploring their thinking.'

Judgement: 'Well done, you handled that well.'

Behaviour: 'You remained calm, despite the challenges, asked open questions that revealed the real reasons behind the problems and played back what you had heard to check your understanding.'

During the ensuing five years, we added to and refined the data and have continued to do so to this very day, keeping it current and relevant with businesses in a wide range of sectors, across the globe and many hundreds of leaders.

This chapter describes each of the dimensions in turn, together with the supporting behaviours and a narrative description of each dimension. It is important to stress that throughout our 15 years of compiling and using this research, no remote leader has achieved all the behavioural descriptors as high in every dimension; equally, no remote leader has been rated as poor on every behavioural descriptor in each dimension. Instead, as we might expect, leaders have had a propensity to be more on high or more on poor, or, as is most common, a propensity to be at the average. Even for the highest performers, assessed by their business results and line director/direct reports' corroboration, there were behaviours judged to be in the average or even poor category at times and vice versa for some of the poorer performers, though in the many, many years of studying remote leaders, it has been very rare for a poorer performer to achieve behaviours in any of the high-performing indicators.

Direction

High Performance	Average Performance	Poor Performance
Vision/direction of the division/region is clear to all. Everyone knows what the division/region is striving for above and beyond the existing KPIs (Key Performance Indicators)	Vision/direction focuses on addressing the existing KPIs; no real sense of achieving on any broader front	Vision/direction lurches from the latest 'hot' KPI to the next one
Across the division/region there is a common understanding of what it stands for, which is actively demonstrated by each site leader and their team	Creates a vision/direction for the division/region that is understood in terms of intent but has very little effect in store	There is no common understanding of what the division/region is striving to achieve and this is reflected in local site behaviour
Sets a clear direction in a way that encourages others to own and strive for success	Sets a clear direction in a way that others understand and are content to follow	Sets a clear direction, which others see as the remote leader's and are even fearful of the consequences
As the role evolves, they tend to shape it and rise to the challenge	Continue to do things in the way they've always done it	Don't tend to believe that things are moving on, constantly playing catch-up without realizing it

Direction

Having clarity about where a region, country, division or area is heading, over and above the corporate direction, is fundamental for success as a remote leader. This clear view of direction allows individuals and teams to select appropriate behaviour and enables them to make daily decisions in light of the stated direction. Furthermore, it enables everyone to understand how they should behave and perform.

The focus on direction encourages a mindset and outlook whereby individuals actively consider and gain clarity on what it is being sought to be achieved, rather than merely becoming immersed in the various activities of the doing. Clarity of direction is not a list of tasks to be completed but a picture of where we're heading and what is being sought to be achieved. Furthermore, all too often individuals confuse what they are seeking to achieve with the metric they are being measured by. For example, I have often heard leaders talk about their direction as:

'to achieve x amount of sales'

This statement provides no indication of direction, i.e. where the function is heading; it merely provides a metric. By contrast:

'to be the business that people think of first and come back to us to buy, time and time again'

(… as provided by a prominent leader in a well-known retail business). This statement provides an implicit business direction, which can be made explicit through the creation of strategy, which builds the business reputation, positions it in the market, attracts and retains customers, which can be measured by a number of metrics:

- sales;
- margin;
- customer footfall or online visits;
- conversion rates;
- customer retention.

Below are examples, which allow strategies to follow:

Automotive: 'An x vehicle outside every home in the country.'

Marketing: 'Every journalist writes positive articles about product x.'

Retail: 'To be the destination that everyone wants to come and buy x from.'

Finance: 'To fund the right investments that secure both our short- and long-term future.'

Telecoms: 'For customers to regard us as the one and only provider of x in the market.'

Achieving v. doing

The dimension of direction is often challenging for many leaders as they become so embroiled in the doing, they lose sight of where the 'doing' is actually taking them. Equally, the business is so overrun with the doing, rarely do individuals step back and consider which of the activities are truly leading to achieving the direction and which, on reflection, contribute little or nothing to that direction, but have somehow become part of normal working practices and are never questioned.

We have often asked leaders 'What have you done this week?' and they recite at length a plethora of activities. We have then asked 'What have you achieved?' and we are often met by silence as they ponder and wonder 'What, in reality, has been achieved from all the "doing" that week?'

How much of what they have undertaken has really contributed to the espoused direction? How much progress have they really made? Unfortunately, there are many activities, layered upon activities, which have minimal returns, if only leaders gave themselves enough time to stand back and objectively assess what is happening around them.

KPIs

This dimension also examines KPIs (Key Performance Indicators). We've noticed that businesses often swamp leaders with a vast array of KPIs in the mistaken belief that this will drive performance. Instead, most drive behaviour towards the KPIs, which in itself does not necessarily lend itself to high performance and often encourages behaviour that has no direct bearing on overall business performance.

For example, a well-known retailer had as a key metric customer awareness of a particular product. This was such a focus that customers were contacted after the purchase to ascertain whether the product was discussed. Customer awareness was a metric and therefore drove staff to meet this metric and ensured they raised customer awareness. However, conversion of awareness to sales was low, but staff weren't measured against this and there seemed to be little concern with conversion rates and actual sales. Teams were focused instead on gaining customer awareness hit rates.

As mentioned above, businesses often swamp leaders and their teams with so many metrics that rather than creating clarity of direction, it tends to create fog, as not all KPIs are key. In reality, four or five Key Performance Indicators for a region, division or function should be sufficient to provide real clarity and focus. We often ask leaders how many KPIs their part of the business has. Their response is often in double figures. We then ask how many Performance Indicators (PIs) there are and most look thoughtful, before replying, 'we don't have any'. But how can every performance indicator be key?

Linked to this, one of the poor-performing indicators is 'vision/direction lurches from the latest "hot" KPI to the next one'. This results in individuals and teams chasing KPIs rather than focusing upon the outcome. The KPI itself is a barometer on the route to success, not the end itself.

Commerciality and breadth of thinking

High Performance	Average Performance	Poor Performance
Looks for and spots commercial opportunities before they arise and quick to capitalize on them	Takes commercial opportunities as they arise	Plays it safe with commercial opportunities, seeing how others go first
Objectively and dispassionately analyses market data providing insightful views and thinking	Analysis of market data tends to show the obvious rather than demonstrate deeper insight	Analysis of market data tends to be skewed by own assumptions and beliefs
Has a grasp of issues at not just a local, regional or divisional level, but a broader business and market perspective	Tends to look at issues from a local, regional/divisional perspective	Tends to follow the current flavour-of-the-month issues
Is seen as breaking new ground with their thinking, setting the benchmark for others to follow	Seen as a safe pair of hands, reliable but rarely setting the world alight with their thinking	Seen as chasing to keep up with others in their thought process
Talks with confidence and accuracy about the wider business and trading environment	Knowledge and insights tend to be limited to this business	Tends to be quite parochial in their knowledge

Commerciality and breadth of thinking

Commerciality isn't about the ability to make a quick buck or short-term gain; it is about the ability to make decisions that make or save money in a sustainable way, meaning one that doesn't potentially damage the company brand or reputation in any way whatsoever and thereby secures the business's position not just for the short term but also the intermediate or even long term.

There are numerous examples of individuals in businesses who make commercial decisions that they consider to be in the best interests of the company. But they often fail to take into account the wider view and some have little or no regard for how their decisions might be perceived by customers, media and not least, fellow employees – showing a lack of understanding of the underlying commercial ramifications.

In essence, everything in business has an underlying commercial impact. It either makes or loses money. Every action has a return, the fundamental question is always 'Does the return outweigh the investment in all aspects, including pure cost, individuals' time and the lost opportunities in other investments?'

From our work, most leaders regard themselves as having commercial acumen, pointing to sales or cost savings to substantiate their claims; in truth, few are able to match all of the indicators in high performing. Many mistakenly believe that being commercial is knowing their numbers or being able to negotiate a deal. Few are really able to stand back and look at the broader commercial opportunities surrounding their region/division and countries. Those who do spot opportunities often feel restricted by company processes and procedures and are concerned with being declared a risk-taker or maverick. In many ways, individuals are rewarded in large businesses for conforming and complying rather than thinking and innovating commercially. Although most organizations would state they want thinkers and innovators at every level, day-to-day behaviour in businesses often encourages risk adversity, compliance and implementation of decisions made elsewhere. Ironically, those closest to the customer are the ears of the company – they hear what the customer likes and dislikes and understand their thinking. They are close to the reality, rather than analysing data from afar. Certainly, quantitative data is essential in the form of metrics, but so too is qualitative data from the frontline. In a well-known fashion retailer, sales staff would know immediately when new stock arrived, which would and wouldn't sell. Their daily dialogues with customers gave them unparalleled commercial insight. However, rarely were these dialogues harnessed by those making the buying decisions.

Having stated that so many leaders can feel constrained to grasp commercial opportunities for fear of the consequences, we have observed many so doing, but they have done so through first influencing those around them, rather than acting impulsively and potentially recklessly.

'Looks for and spots commercial opportunities before they arrive and quick to capitalize on them'

The first descriptor requires an understanding of not just what customers say they want, but also what they don't like. In truth, many customers are more able to articulate a problem rather than a solution. It is the commercial leader's challenge to find the way forward. Those customers who are able to describe what they want or would like are all too often contrasting your offering with what has been offered elsewhere, i.e. benchmarking rather than identifying a potential gap in the market. Real commercial acumen is reflecting upon and understanding where that gap is and how to capitalize upon this in a viable way. For example, the Apple iPad grew from individuals' dissatisfaction with the complexity and reliability of its forerunners with various tablets using styluses or pens, not from individual suggestions for the iPad itself.

Over the years in our work, we have seen numerous examples of individuals 'spotting commercial opportunities before they arise and are quick to capitalize upon them'.

Example 1

In the travel sector, a major UK operator renowned for guiding large groups of tourists on daily coach tours through the Far East had the inevitable border checks, which required queuing for two to three hours for visas. Unfortunately, this country was unable to provide pre-visa authorization through an online facility. This process had become custom and practice over many years and a chore that individuals had accepted. One local leader decided to explore the possibility of pre-authorizing visas for their party group and despite the bureaucratic hurdles, they were undaunted by the challenges. After many months of work, the leader eventually managed a breakthrough and achieved dispensation for pre-authorization. The process worked so well and actually eased the pressure on the border guards so much that they were able to extend this service to other tour operators. Two years on, it had grown to be a self-standing, highly successful business in its own right, now offering pre-authorized visas across the whole region, which has, in subsequent years, become the norm. This was achieved because of the ingenuity, patience and above all determination of the local leader to grasp the problem and make it easier for customers and the business alike to travel.

Example 2

A director was making a visit to one of their sites and noticed a small development taking place on the approach road, at this stage merely footings. The unit manager showed little interest in this and was more preoccupied with how his site was trading and what was happening in the surrounding area. The director, however, was always commercially curious and always looking at commerciality in the wider context of not just what was going on within the site but also trends and opportunities around the wider area.

From his curiosity, it transpired that a competitor was opening a small drive-through facility, which could directly compete with a number of products the site offered. The director's curiosity had enabled him to elicit vital data and he gathered a team together to discuss a strategy to compete, not just when it opened but in the here and now. This resulted in product reviews, a re-evaluation of marketing and increased loyalty incentives, which all served to limit the impact of the drive-through.

This example demonstrates the best and worst in commerciality; it is clearly a great example of commercial curiosity unlocking opportunities but equally highlights the internal focus so many site leaders have and how blinkered they can be to what is happening around them.

Example 3

On a regional visit, a leader was quick to share the problem of the local community – company closures, redundancies, reduced spend were all going to impact on business performance. The regional lead agreed that this could be the case, particularly if they had the mindset of problem and pessimism rather than the mindset of opportunity. The individual began to listen to the regional leader as he acknowledged the potential challenge but also saw a potential opportunity. Certainly, individuals wouldn't necessarily be making larger, high-investment purchases but equally many were flush with new, disposable income and would want to bring some enjoyment to the potentially troubling times ahead. As a result, the local lead was stimulated to explore how they and their team could provide services/products to the local community that would support smaller projects.

This example demonstrates that commerciality isn't just about the skills to make a good commercial decision but must be combined with a mindset and outlook that sees opportunities rather than problems.

'Objectively and dispassionately analyses market data, providing insightful views and thinking'

In today's world, everyone is being surrounded with data and having to wade their way through it to try and find real meaning to make great decisions. Everywhere there are webinars, vlogs, blogs and articles all featuring the latest progress in artificial intelligence (AI) and robotics. In business, there are endless sets of data being produced in relentless pursuit of how this new data, AI and robotics can steal a march on the market. However, the ability to dispassionately and objectively analyse that data to provide insight is the real challenge.

Historically, data was always available at individuals' fingertips, that data being qualitative information and the first-hand experiences of those closest to the customer. Nevertheless, as the world has become more sophisticated, so too has quantitative data developed and been given pre-eminence over qualitative data. As highlighted earlier, the frontline staff in the well-known fashion retailer instinctively knew which of the new stock would sell through their daily dialogues with customers, but their insights were rarely factored into the decision-making process.

The second behavioural indicator in this dimension has proved to be a particularly tough challenge for many leaders in terms of standing back and objectively, dispassionately and unemotionally analysing a situation. This tends to be less of a problem when examining someone else's situation and it seems relatively easy to spot the issues and trends. However, when it requires individuals to examine their own part of the business, the objectivity and dispassionate analysis becomes blurred by an intimate and distorted understanding of the situation, the nature of the individuals involved, the market and the priorities that cause the data not to be examined in its pure sense but through their own lens. As a result, allowances are made and issues accepted, which might not be the case if they were truly able to objectively and dispassionately analyse all the data, both quantitatively and qualitatively.

Managing performance

High Performance	Average Performance	Poor Performance
Adopts an approach on visits that encourages the region/site to take responsibility for themselves and manage as if it were their own business: within the parameters of a corporate framework	Adopts an approach on visits where the remote leader takes the lead in resolving issues and individuals take their cues from them	Adopts an approach on visits that creates dependency upon them as the remote leader. Individuals turn to the remote leader to decide the outcomes and determine what should happen
Creates an environment where individuals and teams are inspired and motivated to exceed expectations	Creates an environment where individuals and teams seek to deliver the remote leader's requirements	Creates an environment in that individuals and teams are focused on not getting it wrong, rather than getting it right or even excelling
Conducts visits in a way that helps individuals and teams to successfully identify and resolve issues for themselves	Conducts visits in ways that mean the primary responsibility for identifying and solving issues rests with the remote leader	Conducts visits in a way that puts the remote leader at the centre of attention

Managing performance (cont.)

High Performance	Average Performance	Poor Performance
Creates a self-standing approach, which means that individuals and teams can continue to resolve issues themselves, long after the remote leader has left. For example: • staff/local management lead visits; • staff/local management set the agenda; • uses the remote leader as a resource to aid their thinking.	Creates an environment where individuals and teams try to second-guess and anticipate the remote leader's agenda rather than clarify for themselves what they need to achieve	Visits are managed to create a false picture of the realities of the site, i.e. not presenting the store as the customer would normally see it, extra staff, cleaned, difficult areas avoided
Holds others to account in a way that engages, inspires and enthuses them	Holds others to account in a way which leads others to fear the consequences	Is sporadic and inconsistent in holding others to account
Remote leader is proactive in seeking challenge and feedback; constantly seeks to learn; pushes and stretches all those who work for them	Remote leader is selective about the feedback they take on from others; can be defensive or in denial; tends to turn to the same team members when new opportunities arise	Remote leader says the right things but does not show any sign of listening or learning. Takes a lot on themselves, delegating elements of stretch activities but retaining control

Managing performance

The fundamentals of managing performance in a single-site context, multi-site or virtually are essentially the same, with:

- a clear direction and realignment of that direction where necessary;
- agreed expectations and objectives;
- regular reviews – formally and informally;
- guidance, support and inspiration.

From the research, the core differences between the high performers, average performers and poor performers is the degree to which ownership and responsibility is engendered and taken locally. By contrast, with the average and poorer remote leaders:

- the agenda is wholly set by the remote leader and that agenda is pursued vigorously with centralized control;
- decisions are predominantly taken and prescribed by the remote leader;
- problems and solutions are predominantly identified and pursued by the remote leader.

Few remote leaders might readily recognize themselves operating in this way as it tends to stereotypically be associated with an authoritarian/dictatorial leader. However, unfortunately, many remote leaders do operate in this way, but do so in more subtle terms and often don't even realize it. There is no doubt that remote leaders often have the best of intentions with regard to gaining involvement, creating ownership and engendering responsibility, however their initial interactions often set the tone and determine their level of success.

Too often, I've observed remote leaders narrowing the conversation down to their particular areas of interest, despite commonly initially eliciting the concerns and agenda of the on-site leader. This is most apparent with on-site visits, whether directly or virtually – the remote leader can often focus all their analysis and questions around particular areas of interest, often an issue in the wider business, perhaps the latest 'hot KPI'.

One indicator that best illustrates this is that the leader:

'Conducts visits in a way that helps individuals and teams to successfully identify and resolve issues for themselves'

From the research, remote leaders seem very conscious and aware of the need to ask open questions in order to elicit the site leaders' thinking and ideas. However, the nature and focus of these questions can be variable.

In many instances, we observed remote leaders asking questions with predetermined answers in their minds, which has the impact of testing the individuals concerned rather than eliciting rich data. For example:

- 'What is the number 1 bestseller?'
- 'What should be at the front?'
- 'What do you notice is missing at the moment?'
- 'Looking at the numbers, what isn't right?'
- 'When I stand back, I can see three areas of concern – what are they?'

This merely creates an environment of a sophisticated game show as on-site leaders scramble to find the right answer, and places the remote leader as the question master with all the right answers. In effect, the remote leader is taking control and ownership for the proceedings and so visits become a process of guessing and second-guessing the remote leader's priorities, preferences and solutions, rather than focusing on what the on-site team regards as the insight and support they need.

By contrast, asking open questions without predetermined answers has proven to elicit wider data as well as providing insights into the on-site leader's views, perspectives and grasp of the situation, which is at the heart of unlocking appropriate ways forward. For example:

- 'What do you want from today?'
- 'How is the site performing against your expectations?'
- 'What are you most proud of?'
- 'What are the trends you are noticing?'
- 'What are your concerns?'

Leading to:

- 'What have you considered?'
- 'What are you focusing on and why?'
- 'What would you back, based on our discussion?'
- 'So, what are your priorities? Today?'
- 'What actions are you going to take?'

This is not to suggest that the remote leader does not share their own insights, thoughts and ideas, but the challenge is the frequency with which they do this and there is a propensity for leaders, once they start, to allow enthusiasm and passion to take over and not to know when to stop. Soon, they fail to moderate their input, and urged on by the positive responses of the on-site teams, remote leaders find themselves moving from supporting the team to make their own decisions to operating more like a doctor prescribing solutions to one patient after another. With that, ownership and responsibility start to slide.

- 'Holds others to account in a way that engages, inspires and enthuses them';
- 'Holds others to account in a way that leads others to fear the consequences';
- 'Is sporadic and inconsistent in holding others to account'.

These descriptors often create much discussion and debate as the term 'holds to account' seems to create connotations of directing, intimidating and controlling. However, in its true sense, 'holding to account' can be a self-imposed approach, with individuals holding themselves to account, provided they have been inspired and enthused by the remote leader. Thus, 'holding to account', in this context, does not necessarily mean being held to account by others but rather through support, questions and insights taking responsibility themselves for their own performance.

Virtual communication

High Performance	Average Performance	Poor Performance
Group-based virtual communications are selectively used to provide short download or gain concise insights	Virtual communications follow a set format and people tend to go on to autopilot knowing when to tune in and tune out	Virtual communications are seen to be solely for the benefit of the remote leader; they add little real value to the site leader's benefit
Virtual communications are used when other forms of communication will not accomplish the desired outcome	Virtual communications are routinely used and never questioned or challenged in terms of their purpose	Virtual communications take place sporadically at the whim of the remote leader and can be ill prepared and lengthy or are hijacked by visiting speakers
Issues are discussed that have real validity and meaning to all	The value of discussion varies from individual to individual and the regimented format is repetitive	Conversations veer off on tangents for long periods between individuals

Virtual communication (cont.)

High Performance	Average Performance	Poor Performance
Information is sent in advance of calls and any discussion builds on this rather than repeating it	Information is often sent in advance but revisited and therefore does not require anyone to undertake preparation	Individuals are never quite sure about what is to be discussed and consequently, they are often ill prepared
Issues that are not relevant are discussed offline	Discusses individual sites/locations by exception	Calls tend to be lengthy, discussing each site/location in turn while others tune out
Able to communicate at all levels, this manifests itself in their ability to cut through the complexity of information and spot and articulate the key messages. In addition, in debate, they listen, understand the challenges and provide a clear-cut way forward	Can discuss and debate the challenges but struggles to formulate an incisive view on what will truly move things forward	Tends to react to the situation, often providing an emotional response by stating what they like, don't like and demonstrating entrenched thinking

Virtual communication

Clearly, all exchanges are a form of communication. However, this dimension focuses upon virtual communications, whether this be Skype, Zoom, Teams, WeChat, Yammer, Chatter, email or any other platform.

For global leaders, virtual communication has been a way of life for many years and we tend to associate this with virtual visual calls or emails but there are examples dating back into the annals of time. Most widely recognized is Samuel Morse's code in 1830s, and before that cultures living in forested areas used drumbeats, while carrier pigeons date back to 1150. However, the coronavirus pandemic has been the stimulus for widespread remote working. In truth, the pandemic has hastened the move to virtual communications in a way that no one could have imagined 12 months beforehand. Virtual communication is clearly not new, as described above, but the reliance individuals and teams now place upon these platforms, for both work and social interaction, is unprecedented.

The way in which leaders and businesses have worked with and reworked virtual communication is described in more length in Chapters 4 and 5. In this chapter, we examine the dimension itself and the practices that have emerged through the original research.

The two most common challenges and failures of leaders in this dimension are that they either:

1) Embark on the virtual communication without an explicitly stated purpose;

or

2) They become overly ambitious in what they wish to achieve through this medium.

Lack of stated purpose

This is fundamental to all meetings, whether virtual or physical, and so often we see clearly stated agendas, with a list of items to be covered, but rarely is it made explicit what is to be achieved for each item or topic. Rarely have we seen the purpose stated against each item, such as:

Information: to share information so that we all understand what the implications are for our areas

Ideas: to generate ideas so that we can find suitable ways forward

Decisions: to reach agreement on the actions to be taken

Instead, often leaders embark on the virtual communication without any explicit statement of what is required of those elsewhere on the call and what is being sought to be achieved for this item on the agenda.

For many leaders, virtual communication is regarded as an efficient way for them to download information, directives and guidance in a consistent and time-effective manner. From the research, this is not necessarily the best way to consume data, as we all have different preferences based on our learning styles, such as those individuals who prefer to read and work at their own pace, contrasting with those who prefer discussion and debate, while some learn through imagery. Unfortunately, for many leaders, this becomes the overriding purpose and those on the receiving end learn not to interject. Unless they have a really insightful or profound comment or question, generally it's left to the more dominant characters to enter into any discussion and debate. Typically, they are the more outspoken person, often creating frustration with the leader and frequently resulting in either fragmented conversation or a curtailment of discussions.

Leaders sometimes use the platform as a way of commending or condemning individuals' performance, mistakenly believing that condemning publicly will act as a motivator for higher performance. Rarely has this been proven to do so. We have also observed leaders working through vast quantities of numbers that the audience is already fully aware of, rather than using the time to more productively elicit insight and possible action.

Overly ambitious in what the leader wants to achieve

Though a convenient platform for the leader, recipients can find it hard to sustain concentration for long periods, especially for any form of meeting that lacks involvement and participation. Leaders often overestimate and are unrealistic about what can be achieved and seek to share information, discuss, debate and reach agreement on not just one but numerous topics. Virtual platforms naturally favour those who are more readily vocal, allowing others to blend more into the background, particularly if cameras are not used. This is discussed in more detail, with techniques for increasing engagement, in Chapter 5.

By contrast, the most successful remote leaders limit the agenda items and are explicit about what is being sought to be achieved. We have seen different participants take the lead for different elements of the agenda. This allows the remote leader to stand back, listen to the dialogue and provide insights at key moments rather than having the full responsibility to lead throughout and expending their energy on keeping the meeting on track.

Problem solving and decision-making

High Performance	Average Performance	Poor Performance
Anticipates issues and problems	Reacts to issues and problems as they emerge	Slow to pick up on the signs that issues or problems are emerging
Explores issues to get to the core of the problem	Explores issues in a way that tends to reinforce their own thinking	Explores issues in ways that are loaded with assumptions, prejudice and bias
Decisions are made with due consideration of site, regional, divisional and country issues but with the best interests of the business as a whole in mind	Decisions are made based on the best interests of the site/region and/or division	Decisions are made to suit their own local agenda
Takes responsibility for issues and problems	Waits for others to act	Tend to see themselves as victims of the situation, and therefore couldn't be expected to anticipate the issues ahead

Problem solving and decision-making

As stated in previous dimensions, the core of problem solving and decision-making rests with the remote leader discerning which decisions they really need to take and which they let go of, and engendering a culture of ownership and responsibility by encouraging those closest to the issue to problem solve and make decisions for themselves.

From our research, the main challenge for the remote leader in this dimension is the degree to which their undoubted knowledge and experience enables them, from their perspective, to quickly identify both the issues and the solution, thereby closing down alternative thinking. Clearly, there is little value in 'reinventing the wheel', however the wheel isn't the answer to every problem and all too often solutions are prescribed to the symptoms rather than the cause.

This challenge extends to how often the remote leader, and in fairness, their teams, look for data to reinforce their initial thinking rather than, truly exploring the problem to find the root cause. With this mindset, leaders seek evidence and data that substantiates their position rather than actively and objectively seeking counter evidence in order to test the validity of their thinking. This thinking is further contaminated by the reality of a fast-moving and dynamic world, with the added mistaken belief that pausing and reflecting to test a decision is procrastination and pontification.

Furthermore, leaders can have **problem-solving blindness** when they become so used to treating an issue that seems similar to a previous issue in the same way and this, combined with a mindset of reinforcement of existing thinking, packaged as knowledge and experience, limits the leader's ability to grow and evolve as they draw solutions from a very limited toolbox.

As Abraham Maslow stated in *The Psychology of Science: A Renaissance* in 1966, 'I suppose it is tempting, if the only tool you have is a hammer, to treat everything as if it were a nail.'

The blinkered mindset and blindness to issues is illustrated in the following example.

Example

A leader described how one of their managers was the bedrock of the business, had been in the business for so long, knew so much and worked so well for them as a leader. They then went on to describe how the individual was less skilled in managing teams and their abrupt and dismissive style meant they often failed to take others with them. As we discussed it further, the leader tended to excuse the behaviour of the manager, with comments such as 'nobody's perfect' and 'we all have areas of development', which is true. However, this wasn't a solitary role; the manager was leading a larger team. Through further exploration, it transpired that there was significant discontent and lack of engagement within the team, meaning productivity fluctuated. The leader was aware of this, but their over-reliance on the manager's knowledge, experience and relationship together tended to blind the leader from really looking at the problems objectively.

'Decisions made with due consideration of site/regional/divisional and country issues but with the best interests of the business as a whole in mind'

This indicator is not to suggest that everything has to be subordinate to the greater good of every country, region or site as all of these have their own unique combination of challenges, which standardized solutions won't resolve. However, the high-performing remote leaders are always aware of the wider implications of decisions taken locally and ensure that these fit with business strategy and do not create problems for those elsewhere in the business.

This approach very much reflects the ability of high-performing remote leaders to collaborate effectively with colleagues rather than taking decisions and hoping others don't find out.

Delivery and execution

High Performance	Average Performance	Poor Performance
Do what they say they're going to do and deliver consistently, despite the variety of pressures and challenges, often using the full range of resources available to them	Occasionally drop the ball, tend to have difficulty in handling competing challenges, often taking on too much themselves	Deliver on some things, but are often in denial, deluding themselves that these successes will outweigh the failure to deliver in other areas
Plans are implemented because individuals and teams understand their role and contribution and are engaged and committed to what is being achieved	Individuals and teams implement by following clear directions	Individuals and teams are inconsistent in achieving and implementing

Delivery and execution

This dimension reflects the degree to which decisions are implemented to the full and not selectively applied to suit the leader's preferences. Our research showed that the higher-performing remote leaders would discuss and debate direction from above, but once agreed, would fully commit. Equally, they would lead their teams in ways that engendered the team's commitment, even for those issues where there was little latitude or choice. That said, from our experiences, there is often a tendency for businesses and leaders further up the hierarchy to make too many decisions and be too far removed from those who need to implement.

'Individuals and teams are inconsistent in achieving and implementing'

From the research, this lower-performing indicator tends to be a reflection not of a lack of commitment and apathy towards directives, but more the amount of different directives that need to be implemented, resulting in individuals and teams juggling too many issues and losing focus on where to prioritize their time, energy and effort.

Working with directors/senior players/head office

High Performance	Average Performance	Poor Performance
Has ongoing relationships with head office/directors/senior players outside of their own reporting line and does so by working together, sharing issues and resolving problems with mutual responsibility	Works with head office/directors/senior players outside of their own reporting line by exception, as and when issues arise	Has little or no ongoing relationship with head office/directors/senior players outside of their own reporting line other than receiving information/directives or sending their views
Provides insights that stretch the thinking and perspectives of directors and senior players	Has views and insights that tend to reinforce senior players' current thinking	Tends to second-guess and seeks to reinforce the views and opinions of senior players
With directors and senior players 'says it as it is' in an engaging way	With directors and senior players tends to provide them with selective information	Tells directors and senior players what the remote leader thinks they want to hear

Working with directors/senior players/head office

The prime location of the remote leader largely impacts on the degree to which they performed high, average and poor in relation to this dimension. Those located within a central/head office function with responsibilities for outlying countries/regions tended, inevitably, to build wider relationships as the opportunities to formally and informally link up with key influencers tend to be easier than those based in the field. This is not to suggest that the success is all about location, far from it, the location tends to provide the more regular opportunities, but the individual's leadership style and ways of working determine their real success.

Those who approach their colleagues/senior players with a mindset and behaviour of collaboration unsurprisingly tended to forge strong relationships. This enables them to gain insights and understanding of issues on a more regular basis, which therefore informs the quality of their decisions and eases the attainment of high performance.

Despite this advantage, we have observed numerous examples of remote leaders located in the field who through their engaging and influential style were able to build productive relationship with senior players and central functions. These leaders had to work more consciously to build relationships and create opportunities from afar, through identifying areas of common interest with central functions.

'Has insights that stretch the thinking of directors and senior players'

Like-mindedness or thinking in the same ways can make relationships relatively easy to sustain but don't bring the necessary 'cut through' (see pages 94–95) to break new ground – this is derived

from alternative thinking. Therefore, the ability to achieve this and influence key decision-makers differentiates the outstanding remote leader from others. Less obsessed with guessing or second-guessing those above them, instead they have the clarity of thought and ability to make a difference and convey this in ways that others want to hear, for example, an individual focusing upon the opportunities that might be presented by a problem, selling the benefits of their thinking and thereby engaging others positively rather than focusing on the difficulties presented by the problems and issues and as a result creating frustration and irritation in others.

Finally, and linked to the above indicator, is the fact that the most influential and successful remote leaders were found to be authentic and willing to 'say it as it is' but did so in ways that meant others wanted to listen rather than 'saying it as it is' in brutal ways that didn't land and created tension, conflict and defensiveness.

Working outside of their core responsibilities

High Performance	Average Performance	Poor Performance
Takes the lead for issues outside of their core responsibilities, in a number of areas, through their own initiative	Champions a particular business area and focuses their attention on this	Allows others to take the lead and only takes on additional responsibilities when guided to
Spontaneously collaborates with peers without prompting	Tends to be selective about whom they work with among their peers	Tends to work in isolation absorbed with their own part of the business
Once decisions are made together with peers is fully committed to implement what's agreed regardless of own preferences	Once decisions are made with peers tends to implement without full commitment on all issues	Once decisions are made with peers tends to be selective about what's implemented

Working outside of their core responsibilities

This dimension largely concerns the degree to which remote leaders operate over and above leading their part of the business. The high-performing remote leaders have the skills and ability to collaborate with colleagues, as well as the willingness to take the lead on wider issues that span borders. This is not to suggest that the high-performing remote leaders take on a plethora of additional responsibilities and become distanced from the day job, instead we found that they were selective in taking the initiative, but when doing so, gave their full commitment to the challenge in hand.

One effect of this additional responsibility that remote leaders needed to be particularly mindful of is not that they become consumed with this new activity but that their teams become very aware of this becoming a priority. We have seen numerous examples of teams equally being consumed and focused on this additional responsibility, often from a desire to support their leader, and as a result place disproportionate focus on this aspect, to the detriment of their core business priorities.

In contrast, poorer performers leading remotely tend to focus almost exclusively and narrowly on their part of the businesses in the misguided belief that their role is purely about delivering these commitments without any wider business responsibilities. This tends to encourage a more insular and protective approach that often manifests itself in a reluctance to spontaneously share new insights or learning, and as a result, hinders collaboration, often creating greater internal competition.

In fairness, we have found that some remote leaders hold the mistaken belief that competition between individuals increases performance. This seems to be rarely proven as internal competition tends to encourage energy and effort being spent on outscoring or undermining others. In such a dynamic, all too often individuals lose sight of who the real external competition is and, as a result, fail to share ideas and collaborate for the greater good of the business.

'Tends to be selective about who they work with among their peers'

On the surface, this seems eminently sensible. Clearly, working with every peer could be highly time-consuming and distracting. That said, this tends to manifest itself as employees selecting those who are like-minded, who think and see issues from the same perspective and who readily agree with them. There is a natural affinity and closeness developed with these individuals as the relationship often breeds cohesion rather than conflict. However, by relying on these individuals' existing thinking, ideas aren't challenged and different options and perspectives aren't offered. Instead, thinking is reinforced.

These indicators, though subtly refined over the years by their use in many businesses across sectors, have proven to be invaluable to leaders in assessing and understanding their own and others' strengths and weaknesses. For many leaders, the research's insights into and establishment of how the average differentiates from the outstanding and poor has been the stimulus to increasing their own effectiveness. Firstly, because so many operate at this level without realizing it, so the research provides clear indicators of stretch; and secondly, since it challenges their own assumptions of what outstanding is. Chapters 4 and 5 bring this to life with the experiences of eminent leaders.

CHAPTER THREE

Measuring Success

This chapter is based upon an article originally produced in 2016 for the use of various clients in the process of creating more focused targeting of success. It supports the first dimension described in Chapter 2, clarity of direction (see also pages 19–23). Since the original article was first published, it has been updated to reflect more recent events. The original article is included in full, followed by more recent examples and insights.

> Targets: If it moves, measure it!
> The undermining of business effectiveness – Mike Parkes

Talk to managers at any level in the public, private and not-for-profit sector and they'll talk about being awash with KPIs and drowning in measurement and data that consumes so much of their daily lives.

It's 'self-evident' and much stated that if you don't know where you're going (i.e. have a clear target), you won't know whether you're there or not. Equally, if you don't check or measure where you are along that route, you won't know if you're on track. Yet increasingly, that clarity of direction is being measured by so many indicators, some counter to each other and all being deemed 'key', so that the essence of which measures really contribute to business success is being lost.

So, if **everything** is key, then the ability to differentiate what really makes a difference to organizational success becomes harder to fathom and equally harder to focus on. Fundamentally, not everything can be key and when it is perceived to be, focus and energy start to dissipate and become geared to indicators that generally have little or no impact on the core purpose of the business or organization.

There are numerous examples of this across all sectors.

Over recent years, a whole host of hospital scandals have emerged, ranging from the Bristol Royal Infirmary, Colchester, Tameside, Blackpool, Basildon and Lancashire hospitals to the infamous Mid Staffordshire NHS Foundation Trust, all undermined by a target-driven culture. At Stafford Hospital, it was estimated that many patients died from poor care and criminal charges were taken regarding four patients, although it is claimed that the true numbers ran into the hundreds. This was a supposedly flagship institution, not a rogue hospital, but an environment had developed in which the core purpose of patient care had been lost and replaced by a target-driven culture of excessive measurement.

It seems the traditional measure of how many patients died at the hands of particular surgeons had driven surgeons to become more selective in the cases they were willing to take on and to compensate for this, the government became more obsessed with measures that weren't related to clinical outcomes but issues that could be easily measured, such as:

- the number of patients seen hourly;
- the waiting times in A&E.

Clinicians rightly objected to these as they had nothing to do with the core purpose of patient care; in fact, the investigation into Stafford Hospital revealed managers so obsessed with the targets that in the middle of trying to deal with more complex patients' treatment, they often closed down the care and moved the patient on for fear of not hitting the target – fundamentally aiming to tick the box on A&E waiting times.

Further investigation into Mid Staffs revealed that it failed on patient care by focusing on so many specifics, which led to a situation where only those things that could be measured or were quantifiable were given any sustained attention; there was a mistaken belief that minimum standards were sufficient. For an establishment that at its heart should focus on the care and cure of patients, cost-driving targets had focused upon the higher costs, which in hospitals tends to be staffing – in particular, clinically qualified staff – together with the training and development of all employees. The hospital drove out highly skilled essential staff and replaced them with untrained personnel, in the process eroding a culture of care and creating an obsessive target-driven organization that was out of touch with the primary purpose.

In 2013, various police forces were identified as becoming so target-driven that they too had lost sight of their core purpose – to prevent, reduce and solve crime. The *Herald* newspaper in Scotland revealed that police targets were creating a fear of managing crime figures. The creation of targets and the drive to demonstrate that crimes were being solved was, for example, pressurizing officers into applying speeding fines when a warning would have been more suitable, or increasing stop and search, which saw an extra 186 members of the public being stopped in the first three months of Police Scotland's existence. Furthermore, in June 2015, the *Herald* reported that the Scottish government was planning to stop publishing crime statistics altogether amid continuing claims that the data was being manipulated by the police.

Also, in 2013, Kent Police were accused of the under-reporting of one in 10 crimes with a bias towards chasing targets, rather than a focus on their core purpose. The report by Her Majesty's Inspectorate of Crime identified a target-driven culture that was focusing on easier-to-solve crimes rather than considering the severity of the impact on victims. For example, it was claimed that officers were seeking out cannabis users to hand out formal warnings to, and a special team established to tackle burglary had been reassigned to shoplifting. Furthermore, victims were often refused a crime number and the monetary value of thefts was lowered such that they were declassified. Officers themselves had individual weekly targets and were under so much pressure to meet these that arrests were made for relatively minor offences, such as urinating in public.

In April 2014, Paul Peachey produced an article in *I* newspaper entitled 'Fiddling Statistics is Ingrained in the Police', in which he claimed that distorting statistics was endemic in the upper echelons of the police force, where target chasing had led to under-reporting of serious crimes. In fact, in March 2014, four Scotland Yard officers were investigated after a criminal claimed he was persuaded to falsely admit to 500 burglaries.

This is not just a UK phenomenon. On 25 June 2014, in Atlanta, Georgia, it was announced that revenue for traffic violations would be used to fund police officers' pay rises to incentivize them to attend court. It transpired that officers frequently failed to turn up for lesser crimes and as a result, these were often thrown out. It was claimed that there was no desire for officers to change the ways they enforce laws, just to incentivize them to appear in court, but what more of an incentive would police officers want to focus their attention on car offences rather than crimes that are more pressing? If the issue were truly about officers' attendance in court, the number of court appearances and those who appeared at least 90 per cent of the time should warrant a pay increase and this should be funded not from traffic violations but sourced from the court case itself. This is yet another example of using the wrong measure to solve a problem.

Target-driven, measurement-obsessed cultures are not solely the domain of the public sector. Many household names and widely respected private sector businesses are swimming in a tide of excessive KPIs; everything has become 'key' or 'important' regardless of its true contribution. A report by ServiceNow – 'Today's State of Work: The Productivity Drain' – in April 2015, revealed that managers spent at least 15 hours a week on administrative and reporting-related work, rather than actually doing and contributing to business success, all too often being measured on things that were not the primary core purpose of their role.

Many accountancy firms provide advice and guidance, day in, day out, to businesses large and small on how to improve their performance. For many, underpinning their own businesses is a model of measurement that seems to inaccurately measure financial performance! Each consultant has a utilization target, a measure of how much they have been utilized on fee-earning work, so each week a consultant would attribute their time to various cost codes, each reflecting a different client project. Through this, the consultant can see how much of their time was spent on fee-earning work that week, which all sounds very logical. The only slight problem is that the consultant allocates their time and not the true monetary value. As a result, the amount of time allocated often exceeds the true revenue to be charged. In effect, projects become unprofitable, as more time is allocated than the budgets support.

Over the years, much has been written and many accusations made around former FIFA president Sepp Blatter and the running of world football, but little attention has been given to one fundamental measure of international football: the world rankings. Why is this important? Largely, a country's ranking determines its seeding and possible ease of qualification for major finals, so increasing its probability of trophy success. On the surface, the rankings reflect the performance of a country over time and therefore appear to be an objective and fair assessment. However, leading into World Cup 2014, how could the following be explained?

- Croatia and Portugal being ranked ahead of:
  - Brazil, the Confederations Cup champions;
  - Italy, runners-up in Euro 2012, and World Cup in 2010, and who romped home in qualification with two rounds to spare and hadn't lost a World Cup or European qualifying game for 40 matches;
  - Holland, who had won 26 of their last 28 competitive games;
- Columbia being ranked ahead of Italy, the former having won fewer World Cup games than Italy had trophies;
- Belgium being so highly ranked despite not reaching a major final for 12 years and finishing fifth, fourth and third in their qualification groups in the years leading up to 2014 qualification;
- Switzerland being seeded despite being the first team to be eliminated out of their own co-hosted Euros of 2008, then failing to qualify for Euro 2012.

How have these seemingly illogical rankings arisen? Fundamentally, the rankings are based on results. In many instances, these matches were meaningless friendlies with teams experimenting with formations and player combinations, which explains why Switzerland soared up the rankings with six wins out of 10, including fixtures against Brazil and Germany when nothing was at stake, while Columbia won six out of seven meaningless friendlies. This again demonstrates how the measurement of success is misaligned from its core purpose. The clear measurement of the rankings should be results in competitive matches, not friendlies where teams are experimenting with formations and players.

Finally, here's an alternative approach. We're all aware of the challenges faced by and the problems created by the banking sector and the ongoing claims such as payment protection Insurance (PPI), which has resulted in the banks coming under tougher scrutiny, with potentially even more targets and a regime of measurement being installed. However, one leading UK bank, in the face of inappropriate non-customer focused selling, has taken a dramatically different strategy. Historically, the retail bank was flush with targets, measures and league tables that drove sales behaviour that was in the bank's, rather than the customers', interest. So, if credit card sales were down for a particular month, there would be pressure on individual customer advisers to sell these even if the customer had no real requirement for one, with the encouragement that they could always cancel it. Equally, with targets on loans rather than overdrafts, customers would be steered towards these even if it wasn't the customer's best option. This lack of ethics was driven by short-term targets and measures while losing sight of the longer-term picture of customer retention and ongoing profitability and the possibility of customer debt.

With the drive to remove this type of behaviour, radical changes were taken at branch banking level. No longer were there sales targets for customer advisers or league tables of performance – in fact, very little management information is now available at a local branch other than customer service measurement. This includes the number of customers seen and helped during a week, together with tests of advisers' ability to be able to discuss the whole range of options available to customers measured by satisfaction surveys and largely management observation. This is resulting in increased customer satisfaction and as a result, increased revenue.

So, does this mean that target-setting and measurement is a waste of time?

Some might argue that if it isn't a target, it will get ignored. In truth, once a measure becomes a target, it stops being a good measure. The key considerations are:

- Do your targets and measures (KPIs) really help you achieve your core purpose?
- How many of your KPIs are, in truth, not key at all?
- How could you reduce your measures and indicators to the few that really make a difference?

All too often, the plethora of KPI measures merely compensate for not having clarity about what really makes a difference.

Measuring success 2020

Since the original article was published in August 2016, there has been a keener eye on having a clear line of sight on the end goal across many wide-ranging businesses, yet many still struggle to measure the things that really matter. Many leaders are still compensating for the lack of clarity with either the quantity of measures rather than the quality of measures or fundamentally, measuring the wrong issues.

Equally, since that article was first published, we have experienced the greatest challenge to the world order in the last 75 years, with the coronavirus pandemic, which has required real clarity of direction and increased measurement of progress.

During the pandemic, many of us in the UK sat watching and despairing at the daily briefings from the UK government and their medical and scientific advisers at 5 p.m. each night. At each briefing, we were shown endless graphs of:

- number infected with coronavirus;
- number tested;
- number of intensive care beds used/available;
- number of fatalities in the UK in comparison with other countries;
- number of passengers using public transport;
- number and various axle sizes of vehicles on the roads;
- occupancy and utilization of parks;
- even the number of Apple enquiries for directions.

As the days passed, it seemed that more obscure and extrapolated measures were introduced to us. It was apparently a good sign that the use of parks was significantly down – this signalled that the social distancing measures were working. At the point when this measure was shared, however, many parks had been closed for some weeks or had at least had their play and exercise equipment cordoned off. Equally, we were warned about increasing numbers of vehicles on the roads at the same time as the government was encouraging everyone to get back to work but not to use public transport. Unsurprisingly, this graph remained flat. We were also told that there were fewer enquiries on Apple iPhones for directions; the conclusion of which was, supposedly, that fewer people were undertaking longer journeys. This presumed that everyone travelling on long journeys could afford an iPhone, always used one, and that anyone undertaking such a journey didn't know where they were going. These examples illustrate the notion that just because you can measure it, it doesn't make it a relevant performance indicator and certainly not a *key* performance indicator. I'm sure in some way these figures do indicate the extent to which individuals in some form were staying local and not travelling, but they can in no way be used as the fundamental measures of the rate of infection at the time.

Throughout this period, the mantra of 'stay home, protect the NHS, save lives' was reinforced at every opportunity; however, none of the measures and graphs that were shared addressed the fundamental question underpinning the statement: how many lives were being saved?

- What proportion or how many individuals entered hospital and recovered?
- What proportion or how many individuals entered intensive care and recovered?
- What proportion or how many individuals recovered, having been on a ventilator?

Clearly, the lockdown process was designed to prevent or minimize infection and enable the health services to dedicate their efforts to the right individuals, but how successful were we as a nation in saving the lives of those infected? Unfortunately, by not being explicit about these measures, and drowning the UK public in all the other graphs described previously, individuals may have tended to reach negative and potentially incorrect conclusions through a lack of data and the graphs not addressing the fundamental questions above.

During this time we also became wedded to the 'R' coefficient, the rate of infection, which many of us followed daily to see if it had fallen below the dreaded number 1. As the months passed, we saw it drop to between 0.7–0.9. For weeks, it seemed the figures remained static at this level, yet we were getting regular updates on the numbers infected and sadly fatalities, which varied considerably. The R was presented as an unequivocal measure and the number became more akin to the outcome of a business result or sporting event.

However, an article by Jeremy Rossman in the *Independent* on 1 June 2020 shared the views of other leading scientists who were not part of the now widely known Scientific Advisory Group for Emergencies (SAGE), who threw doubt on the validity of the number, asserting this would fluctuate based on the model used and the supporting formulae that were applied. It was not factual data but hypotheses from extrapolating data and did not reflect the intensity of cases in different parts of the UK or in different environments, such as contractions through hospital connections or the tragic case of care homes. In this instance, it seems the measure was potentially too far removed from the reality and the use of an average didn't provide an accurate measure that could be targeted. It's very much like establishing the average wage of an Indian worker by totalling the number of those working and dividing it by the total wealth. As Oxfam reported in January 2020, there are 119 billionaires in India and over the next few years there's likely to be 70 more, but their wealth is four times the combined wealth of the rest of the 953 million population.

Merely adding it all together and dividing the sum by the number of individuals does not provide a true picture of the situation and the financial challenges.

This leads to why track and trace was so important and explains why so much effort was put into the testing programme. UK Health Secretary Matt Hancock announced at the beginning of April 2020 that the government was setting a target of conducting 100,000 Covid tests a day by the end of that month. Many commentators were sceptical and doubted it could be reached, bearing in mind at that point the actual figure was around 12,000. My uncertainty lay not with the numbers and bridging the gap between 12,000 and 100,000, more with the word 'conducting' or as it became known, 'carrying out' – these were input words, not output words. This is not a lesson in the use of the English language – far be it for me to attempt that – more the underlying message and intent.

On 1 May 2020, Matt Hancock proudly announced that the government had reached the target of 100,000 tests and although journalists at the daily briefing questioned this accuracy, when it transpired 80,000 had been administered and 40,000 posted out, it seemed this target had been met. The fluctuations over the ensuing days was not the fundamental issue at stake and although journalists became obsessed with this number, fundamentally in measurement terms it was a distraction. The core issue that should have been measured wasn't the number of tests carried out. Yes, it's important, but not as important as how quickly the results could be processed, decisions made and action taken. The test is the input whereas the output is the result of the test and *that* should have been the measure. For track and trace to work at any stage, accuracy and speed are of the essence.

On 27 May 2020, Sky News reported that 4 per cent of results from the Central Laboratory at Milton Keynes were unclear. This might seem a small number in percentage terms, however based on the government's revised target of 200,000 tests a day that would mean 8,000 a day could be incorrect, or 56,000 a week. Then as this book was being written, localized lockdowns became the new strategy, relying on accurate and quick results. On 4 July 2020, the *Financial Times* reported on the government's two-pillar strategy of testing and illustrated this in an example from Manchester. On the car park of the Etihad Stadium, home of Manchester City Football Club, two testing units were set up – the first run by the local health service and the second by a third party. Hundreds of tests were 'carried out'. However, the results from the health service team were available to local health chiefs within days while the third party was required to send their tests to a Super Lab. The initial results showed 78 cases but when the results from the Super Lab emerged weeks later, that figure increased five-fold, requiring immediate but belatedly late localized action.

This section is not a comment on government policy or actions but re-emphasizes the importance of measuring the right things that truly indicate success, measuring the output rather than the input and how using averages as the target dilutes the value in the outcome and achievement. It is so easy to be seduced and swamped by the mass of data and hearing leaders convincingly conveying their messages but having the 'cut through' to see the real measures that need to be established differentiates the outstanding leader from the average. This is not synonymous with government but widespread throughout the business world and part of our everyday business lives. An example could be leaders' parochial focus on total sales of a particular product without looking at the implications of this and the knock-on effects to other products, as well as the wider profitability of the business.

During 2020, as well as the tragic loss of life and upheaval to everyone's daily lives, we were also able to observe how various sporting bodies grappled with social distancing, lockdown and the return of their sport.

Returning to football, UEFA, Europe's football governing body, following in the footsteps of the illogical forms of measurement of the world's governing body FIFA described earlier, sought to resolve the English Premier League dilemma of how to conclude the season with their own potentially illogical measures.

On 13 March 2020, the Premier League, like football elsewhere, came to a shuddering halt. Over the ensuing weeks, leagues further down the pyramid declared the season null and void and all results were expunged. For the next few weeks, the Premier League grappled with the dilemma of fulfilling TV commitments, sponsorship deals and determining the distribution of wealth as determined by final positions in the League Table. As time passed, it was looking increasingly likely that the 2019/20 season would be ended early and Liverpool declared as champions. At this point, there were a number of options, including using the UEFA coefficient, which was being supported by a number of bodies, notably the Spanish La Liga, to determine which teams should qualify for the lucrative European competitions in 2020/21.

As with FIFA's rankings, UEFA's coefficient is a complex range of points allocated to teams based on their last five seasons' performance in Europe's Champions and Europa Leagues. This means that teams that have qualified for five consecutive seasons, but have been knocked out of the preliminary stages of any of the competitions, would be ranked higher than those that have never previously qualified for Europe but have won the title in their own country, such as Leicester City in 2016.

If the coronavirus pandemic had struck shortly before Leicester won the title, it is unlikely that they would have qualified for the lucrative Champions League using the UEFA coefficient. Examining the tables as they stood in April 2020, using the UEFA coefficient as the measure, the two tables would have been as follows:

	Premier League Actual (as at April 2020)			Premier League UEFA Coefficient
Champions League		Pld	Pts	
	1) Liverpool	29	82	1) Manchester City
	2) Manchester City	28	57	2) Liverpool
	3) Leicester City	29	53	3) Manchester Utd
	4) Chelsea	29	48	4) Arsenal
Europa League	5) Manchester Utd	29	45	5) Tottenham Hotspur
	6) Wolverhampton Wanderers	29	43	6) Chelsea
	7) Sheffield Utd	28	43	7) Leicester City

So, in contrasting the tables and examining the UEFA table, Manchester City, despite having won no European silverware in the previous season, would have led Liverpool, who had not only a 25-point lead in the Premier League before lockdown began but had also won the Champions League and UEFA Super Cup in the previous season.

Manchester United were ranked third, having won the Europa League in the previous five years, and surprisingly in fourth place were Arsenal, who had leapt five places from ninth position in the actual Premier League into a lucrative Champions League place. Based on Premier League position and not UEFA's coefficient, Arsenal would not only have failed to qualify for the Champions League but also for the Europa League.

Meanwhile Tottenham, who were runners-up in the 2018/19 Champions League final, and Chelsea, who in the previous five years had won the Europa League as well as the Champions League in 2012, would have been allocated places in the Europa League. The Premier League's third place club, Leicester City, would have been entitled by actual performance to a place in the Champions League ahead of Manchester United and Arsenal, but using UEFA's coefficient, they would have missed out on Europe altogether.

Wolverhampton Wanderers and Sheffield United occupied sixth and seventh positions respectively and were tipped as outsiders to make the Champions League. In fact, Wolverhampton Wanderers had previously beaten all sides in the Top 9 with the exception of unbeaten Liverpool. They had beaten UEFA's ranked No. 1 Premier League club, Manchester City, both home and away and were in the last 16 of the Europa League having won 12 previous European matches. Based upon UEFA's coefficient metric, neither Wolverhampton nor Sheffield would have qualified for Europe at all. So, in real terms, the UEFA coefficient measure of success would reward past performance over previous years rather than the actual achievements of the various clubs up to 13 March 2020.

In the end, UEFA advised bodies to apply 'Sporting Merit', which enabled them to make their own decisions provided it was objective, transparent and non-discriminatory. To that end, the Belgian league was ended and the title awarded to Club Brugge KV, who were 15 points clear of K.A.A. Gent. The Dutch Eredivisie league was frozen, with Ajax and AZ Alkmaar level on points. Both were promoted into the Champions League but neither declared champions. Further down the table, controversy was caused when Willem II were given a Europa League spot ahead of FC Utrecht, who though three points behind had a superior goal difference and a game in hand. Finally, in France's Ligue 1, final points tallies were determined by average points per game. This had little impact on the winners, Paris Saint-Germain, who were 12 points clear but angered Lyon, who were fifth at the time and eventually placed seventh, missing out on lucrative European football.

The potential controversy surrounding the English Premier League was averted as 'Project Restart' commenced on 17 June, exactly 100 days after the last game was played, and with games taking place behind closed doors Liverpool were duly crowned champions. It is clear to see that in the case of the Premier League, if the UEFA coefficient had been used to determine the outcome, once more an inappropriate measure would have been applied, resulting in an inappropriate decision.

Choosing the right measure – why is measuring customer satisfaction misleading?

Throughout this chapter, there have been numerous examples of the wrong indicators or measures being used. The core to successful measurement is aligning the measures as close as possible to the end outcome rather than applying the notion that the greater the number of measures, the more likely that the desired outcome will be achieved.

In today's trading environment, the obsession with the customer and retaining customer loyalty is fundamental to business success and most organizations have some form of customer satisfaction index, which tends to measure the level of satisfaction with a particular transaction. This is clearly important – any level of dissatisfaction is unlikely to result in a repeat purchase – however, does satisfaction necessarily result in a returning customer and future sales? Therefore, a more valid customer measure would be, 'Did they return and make further purchases? And how often and what was that worth in revenue or even profit?' These measures are typically customer retention rate, the number of customers retained and customer profitability score – a measure of each customer's worth to the business.

This type of measurement tends to be easier for more regular purchases such as food/provisions but less easy for the longer-term or likely one-off purchases. Faced by this evidence, some organizations tend to favour net promoter scores, the degree to which customers are willing to or have recommended the business to someone else. More importantly, what sales have been generated as a result?

Some years ago, we had a small extension to our property; we won't be repeating it. Despite the excellent work, there is no room to expand any further with the limitation of the site, so there is little to no chance of being a returning customer. Yet since then I have recommended the builder on three separate occasions and I know that two sales have directly resulted from that recommendation. Therefore, measurement of sales as a result of net promoter scores is a tangible and more meaningful measure than customer satisfaction.

Many leaders state that targets and subsequent measures are relatively easy for sales-related roles but are problematic where a tangible numerical value cannot be assigned, such as an IT implementation. All too often, these types of projects adopt measurements of 'on time' and 'within budget'. These are clearly important elements, however the main and overriding issue that should be measured is:

- Does it do what it is supposed to do for the customer?
- In effect, does it make the customer's life easier?

This is not just a test of customer adoption, but customer ease. Customer adoption does not necessarily equate with customer satisfaction, as we have seen with the adoption of widespread online banking. Some customers wanted this flexibility; others preferred the physical contact in branches. In truth, some reluctant customers have been driven to online banking not necessarily through choice but through banks forcing that action by closing branches, ostensibly to reduce underlying costs.

So, everything is capable of being measured in some way, but just because it can be measured doesn't mean it is the right measure. As has been shown throughout this chapter all too often, the wrong metric is applied because it's easy and convenient, rather than unearthing the real metric that directly contributes to success.

CHAPTER FOUR

Senior Leaders' Insights – Remote Leadership in Practice

In Chapter 2, we shared groundbreaking research into remote leadership and provided the behavioural indicators, within eight dimensions, that describe what differentiates:

- the outstanding remote leader;
- the average remote leader;
- the poorer remote leader.

This chapter brings the research to life, through the practical experiences of senior leaders from across the globe. During my 35 years of experience in this field, I have worked with many thousands of leaders and have had the honour of getting to know some of the finest people who have successfully led their teams remotely.

Here, the practical experiences, insights, learning and tips of 10 of these senior leaders are shared and I apologize to the many other exceptional leaders who could have been included. I am extremely proud to have worked with all of them. Each senior leader provides their own unique perspective on remote leadership, with their context, experiences, guidance and insights, concluding with their own personal top tips.

The featured leaders are:

Stuart Dale: Chief Commercial Officer, Bakuun.com
Debbie Edwards: Vice President and General Manager Europe, Gap
Vanessa Evans: Global HR Director, Rentokil Initial
Steve Finlan: Chief Executive Officer, The Wine Society
Jon France: General Manager Operations and Property Australia, Big W
Mike Hawes: Senior Vice President, International Human Resources, Avis Budget Group
Ian Herrett: former Chief Executive Officer, Bathstore
Ravindra (Ravi) Patel: former Managing Director, Middle East and Eastern Europe, Kodak
Sohail Shaikh: Chief Executive Officer Global Franchise, Hamleys
Michelle Wald: US Country Manager, Tony's Chocolonely

Stuart Dale, Chief Commercial Officer, Bakuun.com

Stuart Dale is the chief commercial officer for the travel tech start-up, Bakuun.com, based in Hong Kong. He has worked in the sector his entire career, having led remote teams for over 20 years in Asia, Europe, the Middle East and North America prior to this role. He has always worked in the field, always with remote teams and always with a remote boss.

Through his wide-ranging experience as a remote leader over the years, Stuart identified four key areas of focus that have been fundamental to his success.

Expectations
With the remote nature of everybody's roles, in different locations, time zones and cultures, Stuart stressed the need for real clarity

of expectations; he regards this as being paramount, both in terms of the teams' expectations of themselves, the vision, goals and standards that everybody works by, as well as what everyone expects of each other, including himself. This is also incorporated into how they operate, based upon a mutual understanding of this.

Throughout, Stuart emphasized that sales is at the heart of every operation he has run and that his teams need to be self-standing, with everyone having the same understanding of what is being sought to be achieved despite the subtleties in approach by region or country.

Communications

To support this process, Stuart has weekly calls, which he regards as sacrosanct and for which rarely changes the timing. My first reaction was that this initially seemed very rigid but he explained that in the past, he'd allowed other things to get in the way and as a result, calls dropped off, the net effect of which was a loss in continuity, and mutual collaboration and which sent an unintended message that other issues were far more important than the team's conversations.

He was keen to stress, though, that the nature and length of the calls do vary to reflect the occasion. When we spoke, the team had experienced an extremely tough week, so the emphasis was an acknowledgement and appreciation of what had been achieved with a brief 15-minute catch-up. He is very conscious of the mood and tone of the calls.

Stuart also stressed that in a sales environment, the teams are already aware of how they are doing, they have the figures and performance metrics, so his approach is not about meticulously repeating what is already known, but finding out what is a concern for them and really understanding what they are experiencing.

For him, the sales element goes without saying, so he majors on encouragement, engagement and finding ways to help them succeed. Over the years, he has seen too many leaders just focusing on and obsessing about the numbers and not providing leadership around how we influence the numbers – they are after all just a reflection of individuals' behaviour.

As well as the regular engagement, he is also mindful of sending private texts to every team member to acknowledge particular contributions. He has found this has a greater ongoing impact than saving these up for wider team sessions. He also endeavours never to miss anyone's birthday, especially for his direct reports, though he strives to deliver this to his wider teams as well. He believes that the small things can make a difference and a simple message can speak a thousand words.

Engagement

Stuart's leadership philosophy is based upon supporting the team so that they are fully engaged. He sees his role as giving them the information and support they need to achieve. He emphasized that they can speak to him whenever they want, and they do. They contact him when it is important and the right time for them; he recognizes that they're in the frontline, so he believes he owes it to them to respect their need. He also holds the view that if they want something, it is his role to help make that happen.

He also explained that if there's no chance of fulfilling exactly what they want, they talk together about what is possible; for him, it's all about getting a good outcome. Working towards finding a solution together supports the long-term goal of driving collaboration.

In terms of being with the teams, Stuart works to a three-month calendar of visits to his top destinations, but he was keen to emphasize that he'll also go to the least popular as he has discovered a lot can be learned from them, despite their reduced popularity.

Stuart regards travelling with the team as key to their engagement and success. He meets with their clients and in his own humble way stressed that he does very little, but this seems to have had a positive impact for his team, by providing real leverage with their clients. He stressed he's very conscientious in supporting them and equally in helping them to have some of the tougher conversations where necessary, while also recognizing that they need to be seen as the key player as they're there on the ground week in, week out – it's not about him.

Stuart is very informal in his style and regularly sends WhatsApps asking how people are doing. He was keen to stress that he tailors his messages by country and culture. He explained that his simple question of 'How are you doing?' to the team in Los Angeles was likely to elicit vast amounts of information and chatter, while the same question to his team in Brazil was likely to induce worry and concern that something had happened, as they would interpret the motives for the question significantly differently.

Ideally, Stuart would like the wider team to come together more frequently than once a year, but he recognizes that this is impractical in terms of logistics, with 90 per cent of the teams in different time zones and many thousands of miles from each other as well as the inevitable costs in a relatively low-margin business. That said, as well as virtual calls and webinars, he also encourages local engagement initiatives. For example, he put on a summer fun day, where the UK team played rounders in Regent's Park, London. Others working remotely joined a more local office and those in very isolated locations were encouraged to have a day out with their families. The only stipulation that Stuart made was that everyone came back and shared what they'd done with messages and videos as a way of connecting them all virtually on the same day.

Cultural awareness

Stuart emphasized the need to really understand not just the basics of different cultures but also the subtleties that can let the remote leader down. He stressed that respecting local cultures is essential, but also reaffirmed that everyone is part of a global business and therefore we must understand this concept rather than seeing it as a barrier.

In terms of the subtleties, he provided two examples of underestimating local practices together with his impact when working in the Bangkok office in his early days. Every morning, he made a point of greeting every team member with a 'good morning'. On one occasion, somehow, he missed one individual who was on the phone, which would be unlikely to cause a problem in a European culture. He was later to learn that this had created consternation, anxiety and worry for that individual, who thought that something was wrong. Stuart was mortified and made sure to rectify the matter.

Stuart shared another experience of understanding Thai culture, where it transpired that payslips every month were personally handed to staff members. Once more, an individual was on the phone, so rather than disturb them, he placed the payslip next to them. He was then advised by another member that physically handing this over was a sign of gratitude and so he returned to the individual's desk, picked up the payslip and presented it to the team member. This was an example of British informality underestimating Thai public displays of appreciation.

Stuart's top tips

- 'Never do it on your own; it is a global business, people don't work *for* you, they work *with* you';
- 'Too many leaders obsess with the numbers; they are important, but the teams know them. It is more about how you help them succeed';
- 'If they are out with their numbers, it's about me not doing my job. It is about asking yourself, "What do they need? What should I be doing?"';
- 'Build teams that are empowered, self-standing and can handle the challenges themselves';
- 'Finally, really understand your teams, their culture, their ways of working and the expectations that they have of themselves'.

Debbie Edwards, Vice President and General Manager Europe, Gap

Debbie Edwards is the vice president and general manager for Gap Europe, who celebrated 30 years in the business in 2019. She is unique in Gap, having started as a sales associate and progressed her way up the hierarchy to being the most senior leader in Europe. No one else has the knowledge and insights into the history, products and successes of Gap that Debbie possesses and this, along with her dynamic, engaging and passionate style, makes her a charismatic leader, who is respected and followed by everyone at every level.

Debbie, as VP and general manager for Europe, leads teams in France, Italy, the UK and Ireland across their outlet, specialist and online channels and shares the insights and experiences she has gained over the years.

Honesty and candour

Starting as a sales associate in London, Debbie developed a reputation for her honesty and candour. Her passionate interest in products meant that almost immediately she could identify whether a product would be a 'seller or a sucker' and this caught the attention of senior leaders on visits from the US.

Debbie reflected upon this and commented that as she'd never worked in a business before, she didn't have the inhibitions that many had, who tended to dilute their messages to the hierarchy. This forthright style gave her exposure to the senior leaders and they liked and respected her candid nature and the reality she provided. Debbie explained how this has characterized her career and she'd encouraged it in others, because she has seen the extent to which massaged messages gave diluted results. She also stressed how fortunate she was that those senior leaders were willing to listen to her in the early days and didn't get defensive in response to her insights and observations.

After being a sales associate, Debbie described how she then took on the role of sales training manager, training her colleagues in selling skills and product knowledge. Though rewarding, her real passion was driving frontline sales and immersing herself with teams, so she took her first leadership role as a regional manager for York, Sheffield, Liverpool and Manchester. This provided her with her first opportunity to lead remotely and return to the cut and thrust of Products and Sales.

Responsibility, resilience and raising your game

Debbie described how she had learned to lead remotely throughout her career as an RM, head of stores and leader of the European Business, but equally emphasized that with her knowledge, understanding and insight into the business, she had always been really close to what was happening on the ground with Product and Sales.

She explained that in leadership terms, she has always been surrounded by those who could support and guide her but stepping up into VP Europe role had really sharpened her focus of leading from afar. She went on to explain that although she'd always taken ownership and responsibility throughout her career, it wasn't until she took this role that she realized the extent of responsibility and the resilience required, as now there was no one on hand to guide her with her decisions.

Debbie reflected that in many ways, up until this role, she had been in a comfort zone of knowledge; she now had to up her game and help others to do likewise.

Letting go and standing back

In many ways, Debbie's strengths, including her open style, intimate knowledge of the business and knowing how to make things happen at pace in Gap are also her potential inhibitors. Nobody in Gap has any trepidation in talking with Debbie, everyone wants to engage with her and grab her time. She always has a fascinating angle and insight that everyone wants to access and she is very conscious that her day can be consumed by solving everyone else's problems.

Debbie described how she has worked hard to encourage collaboration across teams and also learned what to let go of and when to stand back and allow others to make decisions. She stressed how fast-paced the business, and in fairness, retail in general, can be and as a result, there can be too much of a frenetic push for action. With this in mind, she explained how she forces herself to pause and reflect, as well as encouraging others to do likewise.

Debbie did stress that in the past, she had found this difficult as her passion and interest would draw her into decisions. Today, she manages this by agreeing upfront principles and criteria under which decisions are made; with this level of alignment, everyone has to take responsibility for their part. She explained that everyone has to let go of what they did in the past, despite how much they enjoyed it – everyone has to step up, including her.

'Don't do others' jobs'

Debbie still enjoys Product and Sales but recognizes these are others' day jobs and, as she stressed, it's important that leaders 'don't do others' jobs'. She is clear that her role is to involve herself in wider areas of the business, such as technology, property, finance and strategy, and to provide her value in different ways.

Vision and alignment

Since initially being head of stores and in all subsequent roles, Debbie has regarded as fundamental to her success having a clear vision or picture of where the business is heading and galvanizing everyone behind this. She emphasized that in every dialogue she has, every town-hall meeting she holds and every lunchtime briefing she leads, she links everything back to the vision and achieves this through storytelling. She stressed that for her, sharing stories brings the vision to life, enabling team members to relate to these and understand what they can do, day in, day out, across the business.

Managing the relationship with the parent company

Finally, Debbie described how important it has been to have a trusting and high-quality relationship with the senior leaders in the global headquarters in the US. Through this, she recognized that she has been given the level of autonomy to lead the European business.

She went on to explain that prior to the coronavirus pandemic, she would spend one week a month working directly with her US colleagues on both global and local initiatives, so ensuring alignment between US and Europe.

Debbie understands what's really important to the leaders based in San Francisco. She explained that it is not about the details and plans unless you raise their anxiety but more about being clear and sharing:

- the decision she's going to take;
- why she's doing it;
- what difference the decision will make.

Debbie stressed that she doesn't ask permission, as this tends to create doubt and uncertainty, which doesn't help anyone. For her, it's about being clear and having the courage and conviction of her actions to lead in ways that breed confidence. She concluded, 'If you don't want to lead and paint the direction, it's not the role for you!'

Debbie's top tips

- 'Be honest and say it as it is, don't dilute the message';
- 'Step out of your comfort zone and don't do others' jobs';
- 'Letting go is about having clarity and alignment upfront';
- 'Bring the vision to life for everyone through daily stories';
- 'Manage those above you by telling them the decisions you are going to take and the difference these will make, don't ask for permission'.

Vanessa Evans, Global HR Director, Rentokil Initial

Vanessa Evans is the global HR director for Rentokil Initial, trading in 75 countries, from the US and Europe through to the Middle East, Asia, Africa and Pacific. Prior to this, she was group HR director for RSA, Insurance, HR director for RSA emerging markets and global HR director for Lego Retail. She has also held commercial leadership roles with both Gap and Adams childrenswear.

Vanessa's extensive leadership experience with teams across the globe has provided her with a wealth of practical insights. She is a dynamic and engaging leader who is a highly respected director in her field, largely because of her very practical and commercial background.

Cultural subtleties

Vanessa started our interview by sharing that from her experience, the very foundation of successfully leading remotely, particularly in a global business, is to gain a real understanding of the variety of cultures and more importantly, the subtleties that exist within those cultures. She went on to explain how different cultures respond and interpret the same information in such different ways. For example, a simple and direct statement of opinion in one culture is likely to be regarded as a command and followed literally without any doubts, uncertainties and questions, while the same statement in an alternative culture can be perceived as a suggestion and given a cursory level of consideration. Vanessa illustrated this with her experiences of working in some Asian environments, where she explained that there is a real danger that a passing comment or statement is taken literally and could be acted upon without discussion, debate and evolvement of the thinking, often resulting in unintended consequences. In this context, she explained how leaders need to be mindful of the literal acceptance of such statements, which can result in actions way beyond their intentions. In contrast, she described how in some environments, the very same statement, particularly if it runs contrary to the receiver's opinion, can be rejected and discarded with no conversation or debate. Therefore, she stressed how important it was not just to state what is required but to explore the interpretation and understanding from the recipients' perspective.

Vanessa shared that though most leaders would agree that this is essential in all contexts, she emphasized that this is paramount in leading remotely. With individuals and teams so far away, and the reactions so difficult to observe and monitor, unintended consequences can be magnified and create problems that are not apparent for some time, with wide-ranging implications.

Working virtually with clear purpose

Vanessa has led global teams for over 15 years. Though she does spend a significant amount of her time travelling and meeting her teams in person, inevitably the majority of her team interactions are virtual. Her experience over the years has enabled her to understand how to optimize the limited time available in virtual calls as time zones and the draining nature of concentrating and understanding discussions in a second language, with the added complications of technical difficulties, can limit the effectiveness of virtual interactions. Vanessa stressed that it is therefore essential to have a clear and unambiguous, mutually agreed, purpose to the call and not to be overly ambitious. She has found that all too often, leaders seek to achieve too much and this can lead to conversations becoming tangential and, as a result, dilute the focus. A clear statement of what the purpose of the call is (and is not) is essential.

Vanessa also explained that the conversations can't just be about tactical issues, but more about how they are doing, their growth and development, though she also emphasized that development needs shouldn't be squeezed into a conversation as an afterthought. She further explained that she believed that in many ways their development is fundamental to their and everyone's success. If they are growing and developing, then it is highly likely that the business will be doing likewise.

'Keep a strategic focus, despite the tendency for conversations to be drawn into the tactical'

Vanessa also returned to the issues of tactical conversations and stressed that team members can be prone to drawing conversations into the tactical minutiae rather than discussing the more strategic issues, which tend to be more challenging and tougher to make progress on.

She stressed that she finds it important to discuss what's on the mind of her team members but she is also aware that this is very often the pressing issues of the day rather than the highly important, broader, more strategic aspirations that she and the wider business are pursuing, which require the team members' crucial contribution. Therefore, it is critical to be continually thinking about the broader strategic issues in every conversation.

Vanessa not only stressed the importance of call purpose and clarity, but also referenced the frequency of such interactions. In her days at RSA, she established fixed monthly calls with each team member across the group, which created a rhythm and routine together with providing a framework within which team members could work. It provided a level of certainty of contact for all team members. In contrast, she initially found the culture at

Rentokil more spontaneous, in terms of team members contacting her when they needed something rather than the regular rhythm and routines that allowed the business to be managed in a more structured and consistent way across the globe. After a short period of time, she found this approach to be more difficult to manage and that it made it harder to spot issues emerging, and therefore she moved to a more structured approach while also encouraging colleagues to continue to make contact spontaneously when they needed, marrying the two approaches together.

Through this method she has found that there is greater collaboration, insights are shared and strategic issues progressed, while also ensuring issues are quickly surfaced and additional support is given.

Managing performance in a matrix environment

Vanessa stressed that having direct reports across the globe was not in itself complex; the complexity was created by the unique pressures and challenges of each local environment and the priorities and agendas that the regional MDs might be seeking to achieve. She explained that in such a highly matrixed environment, she has line responsibility for her team, but each one would have a dotted line to the regional MD. She went on to explain that as a consequence, there could be a tendency to create demands for her team member, who may be caught in the middle, which were unachievable. Therefore, she explained that it is essential that she, the team member and the respective MD were all aligned on priorities and resources to support them.

Vanessa stressed that she would regularly talk to the MDs to discuss their and her priorities and identify any areas of potential divergence, thereby limiting the degree to which this impacted on her team member having to reconcile competing agendas.

The nature of this relationship has also impacted performance conversations. As with any business, there are metrics providing quantitative data but the real insight and meaning is revealed through the qualitative data and discussions between her, the team member and the MD, which is why she tries to ensure these are triangular where possible.

Finally, in the context of performance and as mentioned earlier, Vanessa undertakes visits across the globe on a rolling schedule. She explained that when she is in a country, she is always fully focused on their business and creates a clear agenda of what both they, and she, want to achieve. She also stressed from her wealth of visiting experience to be mindful of being over-managed. In the past she has seen her visit agenda so full, it has drawn her away from the real purpose of her visit.

Vanessa's top tips

- 'Try to understand the cultural subtleties and really focus upon the interpretation of language – check understanding carefully';
- 'Be clear on the explicit purpose of each of your virtual interactions';
- 'Keep focusing on the strategic issues as it's all too easy to be drawn into the daily tactical ones';
- 'Balance the global and local agendas – try not to let your team get caught in the middle of competing demands, which creates conflicts for them in fulfilling their roles'.

Steve Finlan, Chief Executive Officer, The Wine Society

Steve Finlan is the CEO of The Wine Society, having previously been the chief commercial officer for Clarks' global business, director of international operations at Marks and Spencer, managing director for Thomas Cook and vice president of HR for Gap.

During his extensive leadership experience, Steve has remotely led teams across countries, regions and continents, including the US, Europe, Asia, the Middle East, Africa, Australia and New Zealand. Renowned for both the quality of his strategic thinking and his ability to engage and galvanize teams to succeed, he is also widely recognized for his ability to lead remote teams and attributes this to a number of guiding principles. Before sharing these, he stressed how different leading remote teams was today with the pace and agility of businesses and that has clearly intensified with the onset of the coronavirus pandemic. He also highlighted the amount of information available at your fingertips today in comparison with his formative leadership years when business data appeared on a weekly basis and sound decisions could be made and persevered with to achieve the right outcome, rather than the tendency to impetuously react every hour or minute with the in-the-moment data availability. His specific insights into leading through the pandemic are shared in Chapter 5 (pages 139–144).

Steve has shared his guiding principles below, which have been fundamental in enabling him to achieve success in his wide-ranging global roles.

Step back and identify trends

In the first instance, Steve explained that from his experience, leading remotely is about stepping back and looking from afar and asking yourself, 'What am I seeing? What are the trends and patterns I'm identifying?' and how do these compare and contrast with what my teams are seeing, what they are identifying as trends and as a result, 'What are they doing?'

In the simplest sense, he explained that this is about asking these questions and identifying the gap between 'how I see it' and 'how they see it'. At times there is a real difference between leading from afar compared with 'leading from under your nose', where in the latter instance the leader is there, present, and can step in at the earliest sign of a problem, but sometimes can't see the wood for the trees. In effect, they can become so embroiled in the situation, the detail and the daily problems that they lose sight of where we are heading.

Context

Steve's wealth of experience has led him to realize that context is fundamental to his success; that said, he also emphasized that this is not about control or prescription but providing predictability and connectivity. He highlighted that, as others have said, the reality of remote leadership is that you are somewhat removed from what's actually going on and at times, local entrepreneurial spirit can result in actions that are disconnected from what we're trying to achieve as a whole.

Steve strongly believes that providing teams with the context of where the business is heading and what we are seeking to achieve allows those closest to the issues to make the right decisions in light of the context provided. This approach enables empowerment and therefore is not about restricting ways of working and decision-making, and he underpins context with a structure that provides a vehicle that means regular dialogue can be maintained and sustained. This structure revolves around one weekly trading call and a monthly governance call, which enable him to deep-dive into specific issues and jointly solve problems. In creating such structure, he is also very mindful that this is not about micro-managing; for him, this is where structure becomes too dominant and is used not to provide leadership but more compliance.

Steve also stressed that this structure is not about excessive amounts of time and energy being exerted in order to prepare for these meetings or him in particular. Instead, he believes that everything that they focus upon and discuss should be part of the leaders' day-to-day grasp of their own business, rather than additional work.

Clarity of direction

Steve believes that at the core of remote leadership is the ability and willingness of individuals and teams to be self-standing and take responsibility. In order to achieve this, he stressed that they need to:

- be clear on the exact nature of their role;
- be clear on their accountabilities;
- be clear on where their role fits and contributes to the wider business;
- be clear on where they stand.

In essence, this requires him, in his own words, to work 20 times harder at communicating. Not the amount, but more ensuring that all team members have the same level of clarity, particularly bearing in mind the range of countries, cultures and languages. Equally, for Steve, this isn't about him providing that clarity in a prescriptive way, but his leaders and their teams being able to articulate it for themselves.

Leadership style

To make all this work, Steve explained how he saw his role as understanding the nature of the problems in the way in which his team perceived them and, through exploration, helping them find sustainable ways forward. As he highlighted previously, his leadership style is underpinned by a clear philosophy of enabling the teams to be self-standing. Historically, he has had teams on every continent and therefore achieves this through regular coaching, support and clarity with each team.

Fundamental to this, Steve stressed his ethos of personally being available to anyone in the world at any time – he believes that it is essential to ensure his teams feel connected. That accessibility means that though he may be many thousands of miles away, there is faith that he not only understands their business but equally, they feel he understands their business with its nuances as well as what's going on for them and their world as they see it. Despite the distance, he emphasized that he is very clear that he still retains overall accountability, but firmly believes that if anything goes wrong, in many ways it is down to him not having the right dialogues and communication channels.

'Cut through'

Steve described his final guiding principle as 'cut through', this being the ability to reach the very core of a problem to find a solution in a speedy and yet engaging way. He placed this in context by explaining that the corporate/central functions of any global business can often be perceived by regions as having the impact of slowing things down. He then went on to explain that 'cut through' is looking at ways to achieve what you are seeking locally but in a manner that doesn't compromise corporate strategy. It's very much about enabling the local business to remain focused on delivering for the customer rather than being consumed in interfacing with head office. Steve uses his 'cut through' concept to engender greater collaboration and ownership of issues across the business and in our discussions went on to illustrate this with two examples.

In the global warehouse business of Clarks, there had typically been different ways of operating and levels of performance between the UK, US and Asia, so in order to create 'cut through', Steve involved a senior team leader in the US business and tasked him with conducting a global review, which inevitably caused some concern and anxiety among his colleagues. On presenting his findings to the global warehouse team, he highlighted the commonalities and also the differences, which created tensions. At this point, rather than imposing decisions or providing directives himself or appointing a global head to oversee the recommendations and changes, Steve encouraged the respective heads of each region to collaborate and create 'cut through' to find workable solutions that increase performance. As a result, the heads of regions set aside their preferences and tribal loyalties and this resulted in a more aligned as well as a more profitable business, with owned decisions across the globe.

In Steve's second example, he adopted a similar approach to the global digital business and again encouraged the regional heads to collaborate to find solutions that worked globally. Once more, this resulted in productive outcomes and, again, he didn't have to resort to appointing a global head of digital to make it work.

Steve's top tips

- 'Ask yourself, "How do I see their world? How do they see their own world? Are we seeing it the same? Are we aligned?"';
- 'Ensure everyone knows where we're heading and how we're doing – this allows everyone to make decisions within this context';
- 'Clarity of role, accountabilities, how these fit into the wider business as well as how they are doing is fundamental to success. All too often this is assumed and misunderstood';
- 'With teams on every continent, they have to be self-standing within the context of the broad corporate direction';
- 'Cut through the difficulties to find solutions that work and everyone takes ownership of'.

Jon France, General Manager Operations and Property, Big W, Australia

Jon France was most recently GM Operations and Property for Big W, a subsidiary of the Woolworths Group Limited, who are Australia's largest retailer. Based in Sydney, he was responsible for 186 stores, AU$4bn turnover and 22,000 employees. Before this, he was retail operations director for Big W subsidiary Masters Home Improvement and chief operating officer for Fawaz Alhokair Group, the fashion retailer operating from Dubai and trading in 16 countries with $1bn turnover. Prior to this, Jon held director roles in B&Q for over 10 years as director of central operations, divisional director operations and director of profit protection. He is now the founder of executive search firm, Valeur.

Jon's extensive retail leadership career has given him a wealth of insight and he attributes his success to four underpinning approaches to leadership.

Curiosity and inquisitiveness

Jon explained that being curious and inquisitive, using questions and really listening to the responses has been fundamental to his success. It has enabled him to build relationships with his teams that mean he understands them and what they're interested in, even if this has meant familiarizing himself with hobbies and pastimes that he had previously little affinity with. It also means they willingly share their undiluted views and thoughts with him. This understanding has provided him with the basis for having full and robust conversations in ways in which team members trust and respect each other and it doesn't become personalized.

Few leaders, at any level, would doubt the need to be curious, ask questions and listen to the responses, but very few have mastered it to the level that Jon is able to demonstrate. During his time at Big W, he described how this level of curiosity and inquisitiveness pervaded the whole business as leaders at every level became more inquisitive. As a result, leaders started to learn what was happening on the ground and unearthed all kinds of previously unchallenged practices.

'When 100 people tell you something is a problem, then it's a problem; when just one person says something, you may be just ahead of a major problem!'

Jon's philosophy is that if 100 people tell you something is a problem, it's a problem, whereas if just one person raises something as a problem, don't readily dismiss it – this can be even more revealing as you may be just ahead of a major problem.

He emphasized how he uses questions to sense-check ideas and plans; he's particularly keen to obtain not only others' perspectives but also to identify whether there are unintended consequences from implementing ideas and plans. From his experience, there can be a swathe of enthusiasm and determination to see plans through without identifying the wider ramifications or unintended consequences of so doing, which is only unearthed by listening to those closest to the issue.

Trust, transparency and ownership

Jon explained that with the pace of the sector, there's always been a tendency for leaders to dive in and solve problems themselves only to find another problem emerging elsewhere, resulting in leaders racing from one fire to another. He firmly believes that when there is a problem, not to prescribe a solution with a to-do list of activities but instead to encourage others to think about it and create their own solutions.

In order to achieve this, he stressed that you have to trust people and be really honest and transparent, giving them all the data you have to enable them to make decisions. He emphasized that there have only been a handful of occasions during his career when the nature of the data has been share-price sensitive and couldn't be revealed, but these are rare and too many leaders are generally too possessive of the information. Fundamentally, if you treat people like adults, they behave like adults.

He went on to illustrate this with two examples.

Example 1: 'cost consciousness'

At Big W, Jon, as general manager, was looking to make cost savings without impacting the customers' experience or sales. He therefore spoke to the finance team, who in most normal circumstances would analyse the data through spreadsheets and make sweeping recommendations from afar. In doing so, Jon was concerned that their actions could lead to a whole range of unintended consequences. Instead, he tasked the finance teams to go to the stores and regions and be transparent, sharing all the information they had available in terms of costs, cashflow and the balance sheet. He explained that the outcomes surprised the finance team – the local teams, armed with the data, were able to identify a wide range of both waste and opportunities, including local sourcing of products at 50 per cent of the cost of the national supply chain. These were insights that could neither be achieved from analysing spreadsheets in head office, nor could they have been identified without being trusting, honest and transparent.

Example 2: 'business rates'

In Example 2, business rates were spiralling unprecedentedly, to a point where trading was made almost unviable. Through forging open relationships with landlords and sharing the business dilemma, Jon negotiated a number of rent discounts and rent-free periods in critically underperforming stores. He also listened to their comments about under-investment by the business and agreed to re-invest savings accordingly to help improve the store environment and drive sales. A team approach with commitments on both sides bought the business time and helped the recovery programme. Exit/re-sizing options were offered by a number of landlords across the estate, which he and his team duly considered and accepted as they were mutually beneficial.

Jon was clear, transparent, but unemotive. As a result, the business received rent-free periods and reductions across the portfolio.

Truly two-way communication process

Jon firmly believes that it's essential to get common, undiluted messages to those at the frontline. Without this, teams at every level can lose sight of what the business stands for and where the business is heading. He went on to explain that he'd used all the traditional mechanisms – videos, conferences and conference calls – but found it all too one-way so he introduced a scheme called 'Tell Jon', with everyone at every level encouraged to raise anything with him through an email, WhatsApp message or in person.

'Tell Jon'

This wasn't some form of 'neighbourhood watch' but a sharing of what individuals were generally concerned with, unsure about or even identifying potential opportunities. Jon went on to explain that he heard about everything, from product issues through to working practices and even the toilets! Behind the scenes, he assembled a dedicated team, whose sole purpose was to look into every issue, resolve it and tell Jon. In his own words, Jon became the 'good guy' but he was quick to give credit and let it be known who was actually resolving the issues.

The momentum built and so many practical issues and improvements were made that the 'Tell Jon' approach was adopted by the commercial/buying director. The whole business became open, transparent and solution orientated. Underpinning this whole process was Jon's practical philosophy of:

- How could things be done better?
- What is stopping you doing it?
- Don't seek permission, seek forgiveness.

Jon stated that in his experience, most people will tell you what the issues are but few will take responsibility without encouragement and few think 'What can I do about it?' So, unless you create the environment of curiosity, inquisitiveness and true responsibility, the culture will remain the same. He concluded that if you wait until there is a crisis, it's too late as it's not become part of individuals' DNA.

Example 3: 'footwear sales in Darwin'

In the first 12 months, Jon visited every one of the 186 stores in Australia, which surprised some staff members, as they hadn't had a visit from anyone in head office for over eight years. Jon shared an example from one such visit to the Darwin store, where he met a sales assistant. Familiar with seeing Jon through 'Tell Jon', she was very comfortable talking to him and mentioned in passing that after every shoe sale, she was left with excessive amounts of larger-sized stock.

This prodded Jon's inquisitiveness and the next day he spoke with the footwear buyer, who explained that through custom and practice, each store was forwarded a standardized box of products and this was calculated against the average foot sizes across Australia. This measurement was taken every year and the buyer explained that the average foot size hadn't changed in 15 years. With this, Jon's curiosity was triggered further and he asked if there were any regional differences. The buyer seemed surprised but then investigated this notion and found that the average Northern Territories sizes were smaller than those of other regions; the same was also true for Western Australia. The buyer immediately changed all deliveries and saved the business many hundreds of thousands of dollars in marked-down stock. In response to this, Jon was quick to give the sales assistant who had raised the issue widespread recognition and in fact she became a national hero within the business. He equally credited the buyer who had undertaken the investigative work.

Recognition: 'the most understated leadership skill'

Following on and linked to this, Jon stated that he believes that recognition is the most underused leadership skill. It's as if it's in short supply, or you have to be world class to merit using it or receiving any, he explained. From his experience, recognition is rarely about money but more about genuine and specific calls, emails and cards.

He went on to describe an example, relating how across the store portfolio, stock loss had risen dramatically. If this had been an individual store then it would have warranted a thorough investigation, but the fact that it was occurring across all stores seemed strange. Once more, Jon's curiosity and inquisitiveness were aroused, so he sought out the individual who could help him understand this dilemma and was pointed to a relatively junior accounts clerk. Conscious it would be unusual for the retail director to talk directly with a junior accounts clerk on a business matter, Jon casually wandered over to ask for help. Over coffee, they chatted and shared experiences, which seemed to relax the clerk and enabled Jon to ask her to help him understand the stock loss numbers.

He was surprised to learn that the finance director had asked her to increase allowance across the portfolio for stock loss in order to have more flexibility and a pot for a future rainy day. It transpired no one had provided the clerk with the exact percentage increases to allow for and this had been exacerbated when the FD asked her to increase this further without any guidance. The figures had thus been doubled across the portfolio, resulting in a $34m stock loss. Armed with this data, and the unintended consequences, the FD was staggered and reversed his decision.

Jon hailed the junior accounts clerk as the hero, providing her with recognition across the business for saving the company millions of dollars. He believes that if your role makes heroes of others, it inspires more heroes across the business.

Jon's top tips

- 'Be curious and inquisitive in order to really understand what's happening – it's surprising what's unearthed';
- 'Be transparent and honest with the data, treat people like adults and they'll give you adult decisions';
- 'Unlock communications – "Tell Jon" unlocked so many great ideas and so many illogical practices';
- 'Recognition is the most underused leadership skill – make heroes of others'.

Mike Hawes, Senior Vice President, International Human Resources, Avis Budget Group

Mike Hawes is Avis Budget Group's senior Vice President, International Human Resources, with teams in 21 countries across Europe, Asia and the Pacific, each working with their local markets with a matrix relationship to him.

Mike has led teams remotely in a variety of sectors ranging from retail and leisure through to travel and since 2013 in the automotive sector. He believes there are four key leadership elements underpinning his approach that have enabled him to achieve the success he has had.

Understanding team members and their perspectives

Mike described leadership from afar as balancing the weekly calls with spending time with the teams in their locations and through this, really understanding not only their context but how they see situations and their perspectives on the world. He has regular conversations with the teams, during which his priority is to understand how they are doing, what's concerning them and what's on their minds, as a way of understanding not just what's happening, but how they perceive what is happening.

Local v. global

A particular area that Mike emphasized concerned the local v. global nature of their roles. He is conscious that although professionally, the team report to him, they also serve as part of the local in-country leadership teams, which raised, in football terms, the club v. country loyalty issue and in business terms, the desire to satisfy the local business leader as well as their professional line leader. He described how he was always mindful of the challenges they face when it comes to managing the daily dilemmas of driving the global HR agenda alongside the day-to-day people challenges.

In terms of leading in this context, Mike takes the approach that he is a resource rather than a reporting line for them. He sees his role as helping them to achieve by working with them and together identifying potential sources of conflict, typically where what's needed to be achieved globally might not be embraced locally. He stressed that this way of working, rather than imposing global decisions, enabled him to jointly examine and explore the local aims, aspirations and plans and therefore support the teams in aligning these. In essence, he summarized this as looking at what the plans are for achieving locally and then seeking to find the common ground and connecting this directly to the global aspirations and plans. This has the impact of identifying where the gaps are and where he needs to influence.

Working as a connector

Mike also recognized that the local loyalty can at times mean that there is a danger of being kept at arm's length, so rather than battling against this, which he regards as a unproductive, as in truth for every victory there will always be another battle to fight, he works as a connector. This is not to suggest that he is not in any way firm and direct – he certainly can be – but he has learned, over time, more subtle ways of working from afar.

As a connector, he encourages his direct reports to connect and collaborate, identifying areas of mutual interest and sharing. He recognized that often he has to initiate the joint sharing, as on occasion there is a reluctance for this to happen without prompting. Through this, direct reports learn from and influence each other, which has the impact of moderating local decisions. That said, he is clear on the direction in which they are all heading and what is, and isn't, negotiable – for example, he regards sourcing as a global approach and there's no scope for local side deals or pet projects.

Leadership style

Mike is a highly engaging leader who summarizes his approach as being curious and inquisitive, listening hard to elicit information. Fundamentally, he has to, and does, trust his team but that doesn't stop his inquisitiveness. He has a knack for picking up on not just what is said, but also what's *not* being said by his teams, constantly encouraging dialogue between them. This has proved to be fruitful in increasing collaboration and problem solving, though equally exhausting and requiring patience and concentration with such diverse teams in such different cultures and nationalities and the varying degrees of common language.

Essentially, he feeds information to stimulate thinking and collaboration and regards it as a real success when spontaneously the cross-global teams work together. Equally, he is not afraid to point individuals towards each other and is keen for them to report back on how they've progressed.

Mike's top tips

- 'Really understand your teams' thinking and perspectives on situations';
- 'It's not about imposing global decisions on local markets but understanding local aims, aspirations and plans and finding common ground with the broader business aspirations';
- 'Act as a connector, link individuals and teams together to help them widen their outlooks and thinking';
- 'Trust your teams and equally, be inquisitive about what's both said and not said'.

Ian Herrett, former Chief Executive Officer, Bathstore

Ian Herrett is the former CEO of Bathstore, UK branch director, Wolseley, and has held numerous director roles at B&Q, from the mainboard commercial and business development director through to trade director and store operations director. During his extensive leadership career, he has achieved results through his dynamic and engaging approach with teams, which has been underpinned by six key philosophies, as described below.

Direction

Ian emphasized the importance of having real clarity about where the business is heading, not just from the top, but at every level, and he stressed how important it was for every individual and team to feel connected to this. He also highlighted how this can often be lost because of the myriad measures that engulf day-to-day business operations, pointing out that leaders often receive 40 different reports for 40 different measures and as a result lose sight of what is being sought to be achieved. In response to this, he stressed the importance of having a single-figure set of priorities and measures towards which individuals and teams are engaged and galvanized to achieve.

To support his approach, he spoke of how valuable quarterly roadshows were for him in enabling him to meet with and talk to all teams across the UK. Linked to this, he emphasized that he saw it as imperative that all his senior leadership team were there too, not as some token display of unity, but so that every message is consistent, not just for the teams but also between the senior leaders who have the responsibility, with their teams, to make the direction happen in practice. He explained that this approach enabled any divergence or tangential actions to soon become apparent.

Motivation and drivers

Underpinning Ian's whole approach is a determination to really get to know his teams intimately: what makes them tick, their motivations and drivers. He places a great emphasis on knowing what is important to them, their values, families and personal situations. Without this understanding, he explained that he believes that he can't unlock them as business leaders; it also means that his relationship with them goes beyond mere transactions and enables them to build a connection. He added that this is about being able to have robust business conversations and that because of the quality of the relationship, conversations do not become emotive when discussing performance. In short, the relationship must be deeper than one that is based purely around the numbers.

Ian stated that those who run businesses solely by the numbers can fail to grasp the truth of a situation. He went on to explain that the numbers provide only half the picture. In fact, he believes that leaders are never as good as their numbers, nor are they as bad as their numbers – there is always more to the picture.

Field focus

During his career, Ian has been conscious of paying special attention to those who make the business work in the field, who are distant, removed and isolated from central functions. He explained that from his experience, this isolation can induce a level of paranoia because those individuals would, traditionally, only receive contact from others when something goes wrong. He has noticed that in many businesses, central functions rarely contact the field leaders to share good news, provide recognition and celebrate success; contact is driven more by concern, worry or an issue.

To combat this and maintain engagement, Ian has ensured that he speaks to those in the field at least every other day, often with no formal agenda, but to understand how they are doing, what's happening and learn from them. Fundamentally, these teams, though remote from central functions, ensure that the business performs at a local level and are also a rich source of data for what's actually happening on the ground, in stores and with customers.

Playing to strengths

Equally, with these teams, Ian stressed the importance of not only understanding their motivation and drivers but also recognizing their strengths and what they excel at. Once strengths have been identified, he would encourage the individuals concerned to take on sponsorship roles and additional responsibility for leading cross-business initiatives when it was the right time for them to do so in the business. He made the point that for him, it was essential to play to individuals' strengths and not allocate projects as development opportunities. He firmly believes that through playing to strengths, individuals still grow and evolve but will produce the best outcome for the good of the wider business, whereas allocating projects by development tends to have the impact of 'dumbing down the outcome, giving everyone what they're worst at'.

He went on to explain that with the latter approach, the business usually ends up with an average outcome at best, with leaders exerting excessive amounts of time and energy into areas they often have little affinity or connection with.

Team connectivity

In terms of connecting with the field teams, Ian reinforced the solitary nature of their roles, which he identified as tending to encourage insular thinking and the unintended creation of fiefdoms. As a result, he has always sought to bring field teams together every two weeks to share their experiences, but also to provide updates, obtain ideas and share progress on the projects they are leading on behalf of the wider group. This coming together might be physical or virtual, with the former example the best form of engagement when it is practical to do so.

Ian has found that this has four positive effects:

1) Educating and broadening the wider team's understanding of what is happening across the business and the implications for them and their teams;
2) Engendering commitment and ownership to the project outcomes as they become involved during the journey;
3) Holding all to account;
4) Developing trust, stronger personal relationships and engagement between the field team leadership and the key central functions as they spend more time together.

Finally, in terms of field team connectivity, Ian regards himself as a conduit and filter, connecting diverse field team members together in order that they can learn from each other as well as complementing this by encouraging senior team leaders to come out of the comfort of the office and central functions and join the team in the field. He explained, 'I've always encouraged the senior teams to do this, with the following piece of advice: go into the field, meet the teams that are making your aspirations happen. Take the time to shut up and listen hard.'

Managing performance

Finally, in terms of managing performance, Ian highlighted that this doesn't necessarily always need managing. If you do it right, the teams hold themselves to account. He concluded that when he brings teams together, he is always conscious not to focus on individual performance but instead to discuss and explore the outputs and inputs of the wider team and with that, adopts the principle of praising in public but admonishing in private.

Ian's top tips

- 'Have a single set of priorities and measures that everyone is striving towards';
- 'Really understand what makes others tick – this enables you to have the easy and difficult conversations in the same unemotive way';
- 'The field are your teams on the ground. They know the realities so stay close to them and above all, keep them engaged and not neglected';
- 'Play to strengths to get the best result rather than exclusively developing weaknesses, which tends to dumb down the outcome and the enjoyment for the individual concerned';
- 'Encourage sponsorship roles across the business – it increases ownership and improves relationships'.

Ravindra (Ravi) Patel, former Managing Director Middle East and Eastern Europe, Kodak

Ravi Patel was formerly managing director of a $3bn subsidiary of US Global manufacturing, marketing and distribution business, Kodak. Originally based in London, he was then assigned to Dubai and more recently, Moscow, leading the business across Africa, Eastern Europe, the Middle East and the countries of the former Soviet Union.

Despite the magnitude and wide reach of the business geography, remarkably, Ravi led the business across three continents with a very small and agile senior management team of just six to eight key players, located and based with him. The way he achieved so much with such a small central team is explained below.

Accountability and clusters

Ravi highlighted that he believes his success can be attributed to his ability to engender commitment and ownership across the regions, such that the country managers felt 80 per cent responsible and accountable for the whole region's performance, with Ravi himself having just 20 per cent of the responsibility and accountability.

Ravi explained that with overall responsibility for more than 40 countries and such a small management team, he grouped the countries into clusters based upon geography, culture and language. In explaining the cluster manager role, he stressed that this wasn't a separate role but an additional responsibility that an experienced and high-performing manager took, in addition to leading their own country. The additional role meant that the cluster managers took responsibility for neighbouring countries and acted as a conduit for setting direction, addressing problems and resolving local issues outside of the direct relationship with Ravi and his senior team. The cluster managers were all highly respected and successful managers in their own right and so acted as a resource to guide, support and help their colleagues, with the added accountability for the cluster performance.

In creating this structure, Ravi was very aware of not only language and geographical challenges but also past history between neighbouring countries, such that Ukraine didn't form part of the Moscow cluster, nor Turkey part of the Greek cluster; instead, they reported directly to him. In addition, another key criterion for the clusters was the nature of their business potential and classifying them in terms of developed, developing and emerging.

The cluster framework is outlined below:

Cluster manager	Additional countries
Dubai – MD	
Dubai:	
Middle East	UAE, Kuwait, Iran, Iraq, Oman, Qatar, Bahrain, Saudi Arabia
North Africa	Egypt, Morocco, Libya, Sudan, Algeria, Ethiopia, Levant (Syria, Jordan, Lebanon)
Moscow – Russia and Commonwealth of Independent States (CIS)	Kazakhstan, Uzbekistan, Armenia, Georgia, Turkmenistan, Tajikistan
Athens, Greece	Cyprus, Malta, Romania, Bulgaria, Albania, Macedonia, Slovenia, Croatia, Serbia, Montenegro, Bosnia and Herzegovina
Johannesburg, South Africa	All non-Arabic and rest of Africa
Warsaw, Poland	Czech Republic, Slovakia, Hungary, Baltics
Turkey	Reporting direct to Ravi
Ukraine	Reporting direct to Ravi

Cohesiveness

Despite such disparate clusters and trading over three continents, Ravi sought to bring a level of cohesiveness and teamwork to the country managers by instilling a level of business practice that encouraged consistency and collaboration. This included every leader inputting data into one central source that all had access to, not just for reporting progress but also to see the output for every country. He found that this level of transparency encouraged greater connectivity and networking not just between the clusters but wider across the regions and cluster managers as they collaborated together, sharing insights and learning.

Jigsaw

To encourage collaboration and cohesiveness, Ravi used a jigsaw analogy as a way of reinforcing this and introduced this at one of his early global conferences. He described the experience as follows.

With the room looking at a large table with pieces of a wooden jigsaw scattered across it, Ravi asked attendees what it was. With bravado, an individual called out 'a jigsaw', much to the amusement of the assembled throng. So, Ravi invited him forward and asked him to complete the jigsaw, at which point the manager protested that this was impossible without any picture. This now became the focus and mantra for the teams in every country as Ravi explained that everyone has a tendency to focus on their part of the business, their piece of the jigsaw and just doing their bit without knowing how this fits with the overall picture. He went on to further explain that leaders are often not just doing their bit but fighting over somebody else's piece and in fact, trying to force pieces together that are incompatible. He then stressed that 'without everyone having a clear view of the picture, essentially where we're heading, there is a real danger we compete over the same piece, lose sight of what we're trying to build and have no real idea of our progress'. This analogy became the cornerstone of Ravi's leadership of the region and resulted in greater levels of collaboration and cohesiveness created within countries, across countries, and between clusters and entire regions.

Deep diving on the numbers

Ravi ensured he was always fully aware of the sales figures, not just by region or country, but particularly customers who were contributing the most, especially as 80 per cent of sales were from 20 per cent of the clients. He personally took a keen interest in how they were managed, their level of satisfaction and their ongoing business needs. With engagement, accountability, cluster leads and his jigsaw philosophy underpinning his region's success, Ravi saw it as essential to have daily deep dives into the figures. This seemed excessive in terms of his time and energy, but not when he then explained that without a daily grasp of sales, costs and bottom line, the business could lose millions at a stroke in exchange rates.

He went on to explain that with such diverse countries, trading in the parent company's dollar currency had proved impossible and in most countries, they were having to trade in local currencies. To that end, he had a dedicated transfer-pricing manager with whom he worked regularly to make the most effective business decisions.

Communication channels

With such a flat structure, Ravi's communication channels needed to be slick and efficient, particularly in working through the cluster leads to the countries. To support this, he instituted quarterly conferences to coincide with product launches, business progress updates and to celebrate success. These conferences also served to reaffirm the clarity of direction as well as the jigsaw concept but also to provide Ravi and his senior teams with wider business insights through the discussions and debates these provoked.

Ravi was renowned as a straight talker, who encouraged everyone to tell him how it was, both good and bad. He always instilled this level of candour throughout the business, despite the regional and cultural differences, particularly with a dual reporting line for him to both the US and Switzerland, viewing it as essential for him to personally know the successes but also the problems before they emerged.

Ravi's top tips

- 'Have a clear direction, goals and strategy that all regions, clusters and centres understand, so that everyone knows how their pieces fit into the overall jigsaw';
- 'Create clusters that engender greater ownership and accountability locally';
- 'Cohesiveness and collaboration between teams is essential';
- 'Enable every leader to have access to all the data to encourage curiosity and cross-team learning'.

Sohail Shaikh, Chief Executive Officer Global Franchise, Hamleys

Sohail Shaikh is the CEO Global Franchise for Hamleys, one of the oldest and largest toy retailers in the world. Before this role, he was MD International Franchise for Mothercare, operating in 50 countries with 28 different franchisees, having stepped up from MD Asia and, before that, director of international retail, Far East and China.

Sohail explained that he has worked in the franchise sector for over 20 years and that it required a substantially different form of remote leadership from his days in mainstream retail. He went on to explain that he sought to work collaboratively with franchisees/the owners who are nevertheless representing two or more of their businesses. His role is therefore to ensure that the brand is appropriately represented and not compromised, while the franchisee is focused on making decisions in the best interests of their business. In essence, Sohail is representing the power of the brand while the franchisee holds the power of their business investment and so for him leading remotely in this field is the degree to which the various parties can collaborate for mutual benefit.

Leadership styles and franchisee relationships

Sohail has a very calm, unruffled and measured demeanour, which enables him to work in an extremely objective and unemotive way with franchisees. He stressed that regardless of whether he is leading remotely or not, he has to be and is authentic, honest and above all, trustworthy.

Despite the huge scope of the role and the diverse locations, Sohail explained how important it was to build a relationship with each franchisee such that he understood them, their business and their agendas. He also stressed the importance of meeting them in person in the initial stages. Even though technology had made it a lot simpler to work together and he firmly believes that this is excellent for sustaining the bond, it's proven less effective for forming the initial relationships. He has recognized how important it is in the early stages of the relationship to meet and build that rapport so he would endeavour before initial meetings to arrange for a prior evening dinner. This enabled him to get to know each franchisee, the way they work and identify areas of common interest, which eased the initial discussions. It also tended to make the following day's business meeting more productive.

Influencing – getting them to do what you want them to do because they want to do it

Sohail believes that his success is largely based upon motivating, engaging and above all, influencing from afar. Clearly, the franchisees are actively working for their business, with their priorities, focus and agendas, and therefore the challenge for him is to get the franchisees to do what he wants them to do, because they, in turn, want to do it.

He explained that if he has identified a potential issue for a franchisee, his role is about helping them to see the issue for themselves before sharing with them, in an engaging way, the benefits as he sees it with his external, independent perspective. In effect, providing insights around sales, profitability and brand reputation to help them become even more successful.

Sohail went on to explain that his ability to influence isn't just about what he says and the way he says it, but also how he positions this, particularly in light of the fact most of his franchisees have English as a second or even third language. He illustrated this with an example of a visit from a marketing director to one of his conferences some years ago. At one stage, the marketing director used the colloquialism of 'not teaching grandma to suck eggs', which totally confused the audience. They all understood the individual words but couldn't quite grasp the concept, as many were bemused as to why a grandma would want to suck eggs in the first place.

Don't jump to conclusions

Sohail explained that in his franchise relationships, he has often observed practices that seem to be inhibiting performance potential. He stressed that being significantly remote from the franchise business does enable him to stand back and look at issues more objectively. However, he warned against jumping to conclusions and diving in too soon. Every franchisee wants insights into how they can increase their profitability. However, Sohail emphasized that the key to achieving this is to really understand their context and ways of working.

He emphasized that sometimes logic in one business is illogical in a parallel business as it fails to take account of the interdependent relationship and deeply engrained ways of working that already exist. This is not about avoiding the issue but eliciting as much information as possible and handling the conversation with tact and diplomacy by positioning the proposition in ways that hook the franchisees' interest, he stressed.

Finally, Sohail explained that his considered and measured style tended to enable him to listen to what was being said and not said and therefore home in on areas of difference. In fact, on visits, he has always encouraged the regional managers or general managers to take the lead. Listening and observing in this context has provided him with great insight into the quality of management, the level of debate and their respective understanding of the issues and solutions.

Sohail's top tips

- 'Understand the franchisee as an individual, understand their world, their priorities, their ways of working';
- 'Have your insight and observations but position them in the context of the franchisees and their business';
- 'Don't jump to conclusions – just because a concept works in one business doesn't necessarily mean it will work in another'.

Michelle Wald, US Country Manager, Tony's Chocolonely

Michelle Wald is the US Country Manager for Tony's Chocolonely, the largest Dutch chocolate brand with an enviable reputation for Fairtrade products, which operates in 22 countries, including the

Netherlands, US, UK, Germany and beyond. Before this role, she spent 13 years at Nike in various leadership roles, most recently as EMEA (Europe, Middle East and Africa) sales strategic planning director, Nike basketball and Jordan brand sales director, and NIKEiD business director.

Throughout her roles at Nike, Michelle led multiple teams across myriad locations and time zones. She explained that Nike, as a more mature global brand, had established processes and integrated ways of working, while leading the US team for Tony's Chocolonely was very much a new venture into international business for this prominent Dutch brand. To that end, she has shared with us her unique insights of leading remotely in the two widely contrasting businesses.

Communication channels and ground rules

Based at the hub in Portland, Oregon, Michelle leads a 15-person team working across locations in the US, including sales team members in Denver and New York, as well as partnering closely with the ~120-person home-based team in Holland. She explained that in contrast with the relatively smooth running and sleek Nike machine, Tony's Chocolonely was in effect a start-up in the US, requiring agility, a fast pace and the need to establish practical ways of working. She was very conscious that this wasn't about transferring the practices that had become second nature in her leadership roles at Nike but understanding the needs and differences of the Tony's US team.

Michelle was aware that across the teams a variety of communication platforms were used, from various chat forums to email, phone, video and file sharing. Some team members were always on their phones, seizing upon the chatter and updates while others didn't engage at all. These individuals missed important updates and messages among the plethora of communication channels. To streamline this and improve effectiveness, she instituted guidelines and worked with the teams to establish different chat forums with explicitly different purposes to allow the variety of needs of all to be catered for.

Some were optional to follow, allowing those who wanted to chat and have the usual informal discussions to do so, while others were mandatory, providing business updates and crucial sales data. This level of dialogue and clarity enabled each team member to use chat forums to meet their personal needs and preferences and ensured, at a minimum, that everyone stayed connected to each other.

Team vibe, trust and engagement

With US team members across three locations and time zones, Michelle emphasized the importance that everyone was aligned not only to business strategy, priorities and mutual goals, but also company culture and team dynamic. Ensuring a healthy team vibe built on trust is key to successful performance and outcomes. To that end, she placed a great emphasis on the levels of individual and team engagement, which she sought to achieve through her regular 1:1s (discussed further in managing performance, below), group calls and offsite meetings.

With the hub in Portland, Michelle recognized that there was a real danger that those participating in video calls from remote locations felt like outliers, even though in practical terms, they were closer to the action. Typically, she would have 10 team members in the hub and three or four elsewhere in remote locations. In such situations, those in the hub can often dominate conversations, bouncing off each other at pace, excluding the remote participants and thereby reducing their input and engagement. To that end, she consciously asked those in remote roles to provide their views first to lead the discussion and so bring a greater level of self-discipline to those gathered in the hub together. On some occasions, those in the room even logged into their own laptops to create a more virtual and equal setting for all.

Michelle has always been conscious of time zones (from her Nike days) and varied the calls to reflect the needs and interests of those outside the hub. On the days that offsites were held, they were often undertaken in Denver, New York and Amsterdam rather than in the Portland hub, to encourage greater understanding of what was happening in the field and with global HQ. On these occasions, the local leaders not only helped organize the events but often led the days to increase levels of inclusion, ownership and engagement. Most importantly, the rare opportunities to gather everyone together in person were focused heavily on team bonding, culture and fun! Business results would follow so long as a solid plan was in place and the team gelled well to execute it.

Managing performance

At the core of performance, Michelle stated that she has found it to be essential that there are clear, mutually agreed goals and more so with remote teams. However, she stressed that in leading remotely, there is a very real danger in only 'leading by numbers' as she is understandably not close to what's happening on a daily basis in the field. Therefore, like the other leaders throughout this book, she has placed a huge emphasis on the quality of the relationships she has created. She stressed how much she had to trust the individual and how important her scheduled 1:1s were to:

- create open dialogue;
- understand them and their challenges and how they are seeing things, whether the market, clients or ways of working;

- sense if anything isn't quite right – this is the opportunity to establish how they are doing and above all, how they are feeling.

Underpinning this approach, Michelle explained that she prioritized calls from remote team members so that she was always accessible to them. She stressed that they were a key focus for her. She could see the numbers that provided her with quantitative data, but she was interested in the qualitative insights and data personally gleaned from their calls.

Finally, she explained from a practical viewpoint in managing performance, she not only reviewed numbers and shared her perspectives but placed as much emphasis on the individual's own self-review. From her experience, as they were out in the field on their own, most were as tough on themselves as anyone else would be and therefore she complemented their self-assessment with peer feedback, all of which generated a rich picture for discussion.

Michelle's top tips

- 'Tune your working practices to the unique needs of your business, don't just impose what's worked elsewhere, despite its success';
- 'Building trust and developing team culture are crucial to business performance, especially with remote teams';
- 'Have an explicitly stated purpose for each of the chat groups and communication channels';
- 'Make those in the field the focus for your inclusion and engagement';
- 'In remote leadership, it's all too easy and can be misleading to manage by numbers – it's about qualitative, not just quantitative data'.

Senior leaders' insights – a summary

It has been truly fascinating learning from each of these leaders, who have shared their very insightful experiences and practical tips with different contexts, emphasis and learning angles. Reflecting on their stories, there seem to be a number of themes underpinning their experiences.

Direction and context

Fundamental to successfully leading remotely is individuals' and teams' understanding of where the business is heading and most importantly, their role and priorities within that. With this clarity of direction and business priorities as a context, individuals and teams can then make the right decisions for themselves.

Managing by numbers

A number of leaders emphasized how so many leaders have become obsessed by the numbers and manage by numbers. Though the numbers themselves are essential for business success, leaders indicated that merely focusing upon these doesn't achieve success in itself. Alternatively, as you will have learned, the focus should be on the behaviours and actions underpinning these figures.

Understanding others' perspectives

Leading remotely requires individuals to take responsibility and own issues for themselves. At the centre of this is the skill of enabling others to do things for themselves rather than doing it for them; essentially helping them to help themselves.

To achieve this, as indicated by so many leaders, it is essential to understand the team members' perspectives, outlook and how they view problems and issues. Only with this understanding can leaders start to help team members solve their own problems. Underpinning this is an attitude, outlook and skill set of curiosity and inquisitiveness.

Ownership and responsibility

Throughout this chapter, leaders have shared their experience of encouraging ownership and responsibility, relinquishing decision-making and enabling others to succeed.

Focusing on the strategic rather than the tactical

This chapter has highlighted the need to let go and not be drawn into the minutiae. The more the leader embroils themselves in the detailed tactical issues, the more likely they are to be drawn into solving the problems for others. Encouraging conversations around the strategic and contextual priorities enables them to understand the framework within which they are to make decisions.

Cultural subtleties

Throughout this chapter, there were examples and learning around the importance of understanding different cultures, both in terms of national/regional cultures and as different business cultures. Leaders emphasized the need to adapt and lead within these as a context, rather than seeing culture as an inhibitor.

Connector and conduit

Finally, a number of leaders described how they act as a connector or conduit to their teams, linking them with both other team members and other parts of the business. This serves to increase collaboration, provide new insights and reduce dependency upon themselves as leaders.

This summarizes the key themes shared by these outstanding leaders. The real richness comes from their anecdotal stories and examples, each providing a different nuance to each principle.

CHAPTER FIVE

Leading Through the Coronavirus Pandemic

As I was completing the initial draft of this book in February 2020, the coronavirus pandemic struck and as a result, the need for the ability to lead remotely intensified. This became possibly the most turbulent period that most of us had experienced in our lives, having an impact upon us both personally and professionally. This chapter shares the insights, views and very practical actions that leaders took in helping their teams through the unrivalled and deeply challenging pandemic, and how these approaches can be carried forward into the post-Covid world. It shows how the leaders responded to the inception of the pandemic and the ensuing six months. The chapter ends with a summary of great practice and learning gleaned from these highly experienced and skilled leaders.

Before sharing the leaders' insightful experiences, observations and practical tips, it is important to set the context around the coronavirus pandemic. The outbreak began in Wuhan, China, in November 2019 and by August 2020, there were 23 million reported cases globally in over 188 countries. By early 2021, that had increased to more than 100 million cases in 219 countries and territories. As we all know, this created the most turbulent, traumatic and challenging times for individuals, families, businesses, governments and countries.

For the previous 10 years, we believed that:

- the world has been changing at an unprecedented rate;
- change has been happening quicker than ever before;
- there has been a revolutionary change of pace;
- if you're not moving forwards, you're going backwards.

The onset of the pandemic, however, made those previous 10 years seem like incremental change, as everything was suddenly turned upside down.

- Businesses have had to change and invigorate at a pace never seen before; what might have taken a year or more to do with all the internal hurdles and procedures was stripped away and happened in six weeks – new websites, new apps, new logistical processes … the agility and speed of action has been unprecedented.
- Business have had to realign, reduce and change their working practices from the whole supply chain to the customer, with sleeker socially distanced and more isolated ways of working – working remotely and often from home is the new norm.
- Businesses have had to focus on the security, safety, welfare and care of colleagues, suppliers and customers alike.
- Businesses have had to move quickly to forge different relationships with suppliers, who were fighting with a surplus or scarcity of product. We've heard stories of businesses returning products, failing to pay suppliers; also, suppliers pushing rates, but equally, we know of highly ethical businesses who have forged longstanding partnerships with suppliers to place orders to ease the supplier's burden even if they don't always have an immediate need for the product.

- In essence, businesses have been grappling with:
  - cashflow;
  - financial survival;
  - radicalized markets;
  - new forms of delivery.
- Finally, for years, companies have preached that people are their most important asset – the pandemic made this a real test of the authenticity of those claims.

All of this has placed increased pressure and responsibility on leaders across the globe. This has resulted in senior leaders having to lead their teams through the most uncertain and ambiguous of times. How they've achieved this despite the odds is shared in this chapter through the experiences of the leaders listed below.

Featured leaders

Martyn Brett-Lee: Commercial Director, Welcome Break

Shona Cronley: Global Director of Talent & Engagement, Hotelbeds Group

Debbie Edwards: Vice President, Europe, Gap

Steve Finlan: Chief Executive Officer, The Wine Society

Mike Hawes: Senior Vice President, HR International, Avis Budget Group

Patrick McGillycuddy: Sales Director, Volkswagen Group

Gill Palfrey-Hill: Director of Global Talent & Development, Specsavers

Anil Patel: Chief Executive Officer, Virtual Manager

Jeremy Phillips-Powell: Group Talent Director, Rentokil Initial

Richard Walgate: Director, North Division, B&Q

Penny Weatherup: Human Resources Director, Volkswagen Group UK

Axel Zeltner: Director, Deloitte Deutschland

Martyn Brett-Lee, Commercial Director, Welcome Break

Martyn Brett-Lee is the commercial director for Welcome Break, the motorway service area operator, running 44 sites throughout the UK and with a turnover in excess of £900m. Welcome Break operates every unit on their site through franchise relationships with brands ranging from Starbucks, Burger King, KFC and Waitrose through to Pret a Manger, Subway, WHSmith and Ramada Hotels, plus many more.

As commercial director, Martyn has strategic responsibility for everything that can make and lose the business money. This includes the intricacies of hedging fuel and electricity prices, determining the pricing and margins on products, managing supplier relationships, marketing and PR, and above all, managing the complexities of the franchise relationships.

As the coronavirus crisis started to emerge in February 2020, Martyn, as a member of the executive team, had already begun developing contingency plans and modelling various scenarios, which included hibernating parts of operations, re-shaping working hours and practices and re-focusing the business. All this was undertaken within the context of the business being mandated under their Department of Transport agreement, to provide a 24-hours-a-day, seven-days-a-week service to enable drivers to rest, refresh and refuel.

In our interview, Martyn described the challenges, the outcomes and his learning from leading through the pandemic.

Complexity of the franchise relationship

As Martyn and his fellow operating board members were building their pandemic strategy, so their franchise partners were doing likewise, but as independent brands, each had their own priorities, perspectives and positions they intended to take. In any other business, once the board had made their strategic decisions, the only issue would be the ability of the business to implement these. For Martyn, it was a more complex and challenging problem of influencing and negotiating, to find the right solutions for each of the respective brands, in the context of fulfilling the requirements of the government's Department of Transport.

Martyn described this as a fascinating period, learning much more than ever before about each company's culture and gaining insights into their ways of working. Throughout, he felt he had to keep a keen eye on ensuring that the commercials never compromised customer, colleague or supplier safety. He went on to stress that the world, even before the global pandemic, was a very different place commercially, where doing the right thing and being a strong corporate citizen far outweighed the drive for profit.

Navigating the ambiguity: 'a strong boat that was riding very rocky seas'

Though Martyn and his colleagues could not predict the outcome of the pandemic period, they knew they had in their words, 'a strong boat that was riding very rocky seas and it was about everyone hunkering down together to get through the storm'. He was also clear that his mission was to protect as many jobs as possible; it wasn't about profit or cost.

With this outlook underlying their thinking, Martyn and his colleagues, like other business leaders, embarked upon daily business updates. He described how they quickly came to terms with the notion that with so much uncertainty, they couldn't fill the void by providing certainty. Instead, he and his colleagues stated very clearly:

- what they knew at that moment;
- what their plan would be, depending upon how the scenarios evolved.

They then solicited the teams' thoughts and ideas on a daily basis.

So, rather than predicting the future, they provided reassurance through the actions they would take. This proved to engender confidence and clarity without artificially removing the reality of the ambiguity.

Greater intensity of engagement created greater output

Throughout the period, Martyn described how the contact time with his direct team increased. There were more conversations, more discussion and more ideas as he encouraged his team to think radically about what should be both their and the function's key focus. He explained that rather than let his team be consumed with anticipating when things would get back to normal, he encouraged them to channel their efforts and energy into new ideas. As a result, projects that would normally have taken two years were achieved in less than two weeks.

For example, for some time there had been talk of developing a customer app for ordering products, but the drive and real need to see it through had never materialized. Customers can now order through an app and collect their products on arrival at the services.

Challenged the unwritten rules: 'presenteeism' and 'watching a film at home, while scrolling through your phone'

Martyn also spoke of how his team had challenged and changed long-held unwritten rules and beliefs. It was a commonly held belief reinforced by peer behaviour that unless you travelled at least 1,000 miles a week and visited half a dozen sites, you weren't really contributing to the business – a premise of presenteeism.

He explained that the pandemic had encouraged individuals to scrutinize themselves, and examine what they did and everyone now focused less on the input (hours) and more on the output (what's been achieved). This has meant the presenteeism behaviour has curtailed and even after lockdown was eased, this was being sustained as individuals were more selective and discerning about when and which sites they visited.

To support this, Martyn has instigated two email-free days a week for himself and his team to encourage everyone to be dedicated, focused and not distracted when visiting sites. He explained that in the past, he and his colleagues would allow the constant flow of emails to interrupt the matters in hand on visits and that the pandemic had created greater self-discipline. To illustrate this, he used the analogy of watching a film at home, while scrolling through your phone: you grasp the essence but lose the important subtleties and nuances of what is really going on.

Collaboration

Martyn highlighted how the pandemic had thrust everyone to work closer together; his own team, those across the business, suppliers and brand suppliers all were 'guiding the boat through the storm together'. He recognized that these heightened levels of collaboration and output during the crisis now needed to be sustained.

Finally, Martyn reflected on how he's learned to step back more after his operational experience at Sainsbury's and commercial director role at Merlin Entertainment had encouraged him to tend to be immersed in everything. He recognized the strength of his team and now adopts an approach of aligning the team to the strategic direction and then letting them get on with it. He is now far more productive and more laser-focused on where they are heading, not just this year, but four years ahead, he explained. He is also clearer on where he can make the biggest impact, working on those things that only he can do, thereby making more of a difference rather than being consumed in the minutiae.

Shona Cronley, Global Director of Talent & Engagement, Hotelbeds Group

Shona Cronley is the global director of talent and engagement for the Spanish-owned travel and hotel business, Hotelbeds. Before this, she was global head of talent, engagement, internal communications & CSR for GTA, head of learning, development and talent for Kuoni and prior to both these appointments, she held a leadership and management development role at Nike in the Netherlands.

Shona explained that as a Palma-based business, they had seen the pandemic emerge through its impact on their Asian business and as it moved ferociously into Europe, Spain became one of the first countries to enter lockdown in early March 2020. Shona's fascinating insights and learning are shared below.

Transparency

With a business spanning the globe, effective communication has always been at the core of Hotelbeds' success. That said, Shona explained that during this period, there was a very clear realization that the level of overt and transparent communication needed to increase. There was more explicit sharing of how the business was performing, the challenges, dilemmas and fundamentally, transparency around the numbers. She stressed that though the business did share the financials in the past, it hadn't done so with the level of detail and transparency that it did during the pandemic. There was complete honesty about where the business was and what it meant in a sector that had been ravaged. This had a huge impact on teams everywhere in the business in that there was a real feeling of being in it together. More remarkably, Shona highlighted that despite working remotely, the levels of engagement were higher than pre-pandemic. In many ways, the business had become more united in the adversity of the crisis.

Leaders' adaptability

Though working remotely was commonplace for some, it was not the normal practice for all. Shona explained how leaders had to learn to adapt quickly to the new ways of working. They had to make more effort to stay in contact with their teams and focus on reinforcing the messages around the priorities as well as understanding the needs of team members.

From her own experiences with her own teams, Shona became focused and conversations were less distracted and disrupted in comparison to the office environment. She equally stressed how important it was to agree upfront how to work with each team member by recognizing that the individual had different pressures and priorities, balancing work, family, home schooling and the rest of their lives. She went on to explain how, as the leader, she tried to flex her working day to fit with theirs – even though she too was grappling with her own home-schooling duties and work-balancing challenges. Consequently, this was a time of real support.

Loss of networking and collaboration

The head office in Palma was a hub of activity in terms of networking, collaboration and decision-making. With its closure, it meant that cross-team connections became more difficult and collaborative decisions were harder to make. No longer could Shona informally catch up with colleagues to jointly make decisions on issues or through bumping into each other pick up on ideas or areas that they hadn't realized were of mutual interest. In reality, the natural spontaneity and collaboration that the office dynamic created had evaporated. Shona explained that informal opportunities now had to be formalized through scheduled Zoom or Skype calls. As a consequence, she reflected, 'We only talk across teams when there's a pressing need to and we have lost the informality that held us all together.' She stressed that in terms of efficiency the remote working works, but also pondered, 'but what opportunities have been lost?'

This contrasts so much within teams, where regular calls have included business discussions, social events, Friday drinks and interactive quizzes all designed to sustain both the formal and informal relationships.

Debbie Edwards, Vice President, Europe, Gap

As you will have read in Chapter 4 (see pages 81–85), Debbie Edwards is VP Europe for Gap, with responsibility for stores throughout the UK, Ireland, France and Italy, as well as the full operation of Gap's online business in Europe. When lockdown was instigated on 23 March 2020 and the whole store portfolio ground to a halt, one might have been forgiven for being demoralized and devastated, but as throughout her career, Debbie has always maintained a positive and opportunistic perspective, seeking to find opportunity in every difficulty.

Streamlining the decision-making process

With the parent company based in San Francisco, virtual interactions were common and engrained in business practice. That said, conducting virtual decision-making across the whole of Debbie's European team posed a fresh challenge. Although virtual interactions with San Francisco were common, making decisions across the European team virtually was less so. In fact, the senior decision-making group could often number in excess of 20, with contributions from various outliers. Debbie recognized that this was no longer going to be viable in a virtual context, so to that end, she streamlined the process by creating smaller decision-making groups of five to six depending on the nature of the decision to be made. This entailed wider communication of the decisions, the rationale and the elements considered in making the decisions and was essential in order to retain the engagement of those excluded.

The net effect was that it increased the speed at which decisions were made, which Debbie estimated as tenfold, and made the business more agile to respond to the daily challenges posed by the pandemic.

Breaking the boundaries

As described in Chapter 4, Debbie is passionate about the business, the people and the products. In terms of product, she thrived on being part of these buying decisions, which stemmed from her early days as a sales associate. Typically, she would head a team that travelled to New York City to examine first hand potential products and make buying decisions on extensive collections.

Now, for the first time in Gap's history, collections were bought and huge investment made through virtual examination and decision-making. Debbie concluded that though it wasn't as exciting and engaging as examining the collection in a live experience, it nevertheless worked. The new norm is not necessarily ideal, nor exciting, but pragmatically, it does work.

Take everyone on the journey

Debbie's final reflections on the pandemic focused on individuals' attitudes and outlooks and a harsh lesson on the re-opening of the French business.

With France ahead of the UK in initially loosening its first lockdown, the senior team began planning the new, socially distanced stores and updated ways of working. In fact, the plans were ahead of the competition and set a benchmark for others. Buoyed by this thinking, senior leaders began enthusiastically to engage with local leaders, talking excitedly and positively about the return. They were somewhat surprised that the enthusiasm and expectation wasn't reciprocated. This stemmed not from a lack of commitment or desire to return to work but was more to do with the fact that they hadn't been taken on the journey and adjusted their mindset to the ways forward. The local leaders hadn't had the chance to transition from their lockdown mindsets, concerns and worries and allow themselves be led on a journey that eased them back into working mindset. This proved to be a salutary lesson: understand others' concerns and anxieties and attend to these first before even contemplating taking them on the journey.

Steve Finlan, Chief Executive Officer, The Wine Society

When the first UK lockdown was instigated on 23 March 2020, Steve Finlan, CEO of The Wine Society, had no hesitation in temporarily closing the business in order to protect all of his employees.

With a heritage approaching 150 years and a society built upon strong principles of integrity, authenticity and 'passion before profit', Steve was adamant that the safety and security of everyone in the business was of paramount importance despite pressure from competitors to continue to trade. In fact, as we all became aware, some companies across sectors had chosen to interpret the guidelines to their benefit. They continued to trade despite a level of outrage highlighted in the media. By contrast, The Wine Society under Steve's leadership, though in principle entitled to trade, decided to take stock and re-shape the business.

While safety was paramount, changes to the operation were also needed to keep pace with the huge demand for wine during this period. The Wine Society infrastructure was in the early stages of modernization and high demand required changes to the operation and to systems to enable volumes bigger than those needed for Christmas to be delivered from a socially distanced facility.

Throughout his career, Steve has demonstrated a real ability to combine high-quality strategic thinking with the art and skill of enthusing and energizing his teams and this enabled him to transform The Wine Society.

Transformation of the business: 'internal hurdles and problems were removed'

With people at the heart of Steve's decisions, he first and foremost, like other companies, closed the trading office and all team members began working remotely. To ease this transformation though, every individual was provided with dedicated 1:1 coaching and support to enable them to optimize the virtual ways of working to their benefit. This was further evaluated and improved as lockdown progressed.

The warehouse, which is the heart of the distribution function, was transformed into a socially distanced, Covid-secure environment with no potential areas of congestion or contamination points. Each team member had their own designated working area, with their specific mechanical equipment, and working practices that meant instead of operating an eight-hour shift, the business now ran two six-hour shifts, with no reductions in remuneration. All areas were sanitized fully between shifts.

In terms of investment, like most other business, large-scale capital investment was halted for the time being. However, Steve hastened through planned changes to the website. The website was in the process of being replaced and this project was given added impetus with Society and support providers working remotely to accelerate the re-platform. Like many other practices in the business, the traditional internal hurdles were removed and problems resolved while changes were achieved at an unprecedented rate.

Finally, in terms of wholly transforming the business, and in the face of individuals tending to think and state what couldn't be achieved, Steve encouraged a more positive mindset of what could be achieved. As lockdown progressed, the business quickly developed from being a traditional print-based marketing organization to a digital first, socially engaged business – all part of the strategy, but accelerated during this period.

Well-being and engagement

Throughout the business changes, Steve had individual and teams' well-being and engagement at the forefront of his strategy. With the implications of the pandemic changing daily, he held daily virtual calls with his senior team to provide updates, make decisions and navigate the emerging challenges. He regarded engagement as sacrosanct and while continuing to engage with the business through briefings and Q+A sessions, he recognized that in virtual working, he needed informal conversations to be happening across the business, encouraging his leaders to create chat forums and their own briefings in order to increase dialogue throughout the business. In this way, everyone was aware of everything that was happening at each level.

To compliment this, Steve launched an employee engagement app – Cheers! – which created a social network across the business and avoided staff feeling they were working in isolation. This was particularly meaningful for some of the creative functions as a way of continuing to stimulate creativity in the virtual world and encourage collaboration.

With such a strong heritage, experts are in abundance and the Society converted their classical wine-tasting activities to virtual versions, with customers and staff alike joining the tasting and able to pre-order the wines in advance. Entertainment and engagement of members throughout lockdown was essential and the Society utilized Zoom, Instagram Live and its own community to create a comprehensive programme, with events almost every day throughout the period. As a result, The Wine Society community grew and became even more actively engaged.

Steve also commented that, remarkably, he believed that most individuals were not only more highly engaged, which wasn't unusual for the Society, but even more productive. He attributed this to the lack of distraction in the office, he hastened to add, not from discussions with their colleagues, but more from individuals like himself wandering around and asking questions, resulting in a whole host of unintended consequences.

Operating with integrity: 'furloughed but not forgotten'

Steve's integrity is epitomized by the care and concern he showed for teams across the business in the decisions he made. Even though he had to make the tough decision to furlough some members of staff, he was determined that these team members in his own words 'weren't furloughed and forgotten'. To that end, he embarked on a process of continual communication, utilizing an app that enabled everyone to communicate. Steve was clear that when the moment was right, he wanted the teams to return, engaged and enthused, to be part of The Wine Society again, and not disillusioned and disenchanted, as he'd heard furloughed employees were elsewhere.

Steve's level of integrity pervades all he does. In fact, during the early days of the pandemic, the media was awash with stories of business reneging on commitments to suppliers, withdrawing payments and returning goods. By contrast, Steve took an alternative strategy. Despite having sufficient product, he encouraged further orders to be placed with wine growers in order to secure the producers' future and enable them to have the confidence and funding to continue. While competitors shrank their ranges and offerings, The Wine Society maintained the breadth of their offer, once more supporting the winemakers.

But it wasn't all plain sailing. With a 145,000-strong customer base, who are in effect owners of the Society, Steve continued to sustain their engagement by explaining in detail why he'd made the difficult but necessary decision to initially close the business in order to transform the way it worked. That said, it transpired that a small number of customers disagreed with his decision. Further investigation revealed that a large number of this group had become members shortly before lockdown and therefore hadn't quite grasped the Society's heritage and values.

In Steve's typically engaging style:

- he didn't ignore them;
- he didn't send a corporate email or letter;
- he didn't denounce them.

Instead, each customer received a personal call from Steve to discuss his actions and their responses.

Steve's radical and brave approach to close and transition the business has in effect enabled the Society not just to be fit for purpose throughout the pandemic, but also positioned for the future. In many ways, he has future-proofed the business by simplifying and streamlining a previously highly complicated organization such that it would be able to weather any subsequent lockdown without making changes to the operation. At the same time, the business has been able to satisfy an unprecedented demand for wine.

Mike Hawes, Senior Vice President, HR International, Avis Budget Group

Mike Hawes is Senior Vice President, HR International (EMEA, Asia Pacific) for Avis Budget Group, the parent company of Avis, Budget and Zipcar brands. The international business covers some 20 markets and 11,000 employees, with Mike having responsibility for 160 business professionals.

With the core rental business predominantly linked to corporate and leisure travel, Avis Budget Group ground to a shuddering halt in March 2020 with the onset of coronavirus as it spread across Asia into the primary markets in Europe and North America. Aside from the bricks and mortar operation of physical rental stores, where working remotely was not an option, previously untried and untested practices for mass remote working were put in place for approximately 3,500 staff across all of the international headquarter offices, contact and service centres. Mike described both the impact of the pandemic and the realignment of the business as seismic in terms of the change made. Here, he shares his insights and learning.

Leadership/engagement: 'real humans talking to real humans'

Mike described how the changes had impacted upon leaders and their teams, not just in working practices, but also with fundamental shifts in outlook from a typically task-focused orientation to being more flexible, empathetic and understanding of others' challenges and priorities. This more empathetic style also underpinned messaging across the business as he explained that although there were difficult messages to share, a great deal of thought was given to how they were conveyed, such that they didn't induce further anxiety or panic. Mike highlighted that although at times leaders had to handle tough virtual conversations, he instilled a mantra of 'real humans talking to real humans'; in essence, despite the screen, talk as you normally would, in his words, 'with no corporate speak'.

With the normal working environment being a physical location, leaders would tend to walk the floor, casually interjecting and joining conversations and informally catching up with their team. Mike described how he'd encouraged leaders to create virtual floor walks, by making themselves and their calendars freely available to their teams, so at any point team members could get in touch. He also encouraged leaders to intermittently message their teams, day to day, for quick check-ins.

Concise messaging

The pandemic required every business and every leader to communicate like never before. That said, Mike stressed that there was a very real danger of leaders and teams being overwhelmed with constant messaging, which distracted them from their key focus. To that end, he introduced a practice of 'concise messaging', where he sent just one email at the start of the week to his senior team, containing no more than three key messages or areas of focus – the simplicity provided the focus.

'Go hard and go quick'

Finally, Mike shared how the pandemic had really encouraged leaders to challenge their thinking of what is possible together with what he described as to 'go hard and go quick'. He explained that in the crisis, there was no time to wait. The rate of change was so quick that if you tended to wait and hesitate, you floundered; there was a real danger of becoming a rabbit in the headlights, stuck while everything was flying around you. This period required speed of action and real follow-through; it was about having the courage of your convictions.

After four months of focus on actions required to keep the business afloat, Mike and his leadership team orchestrated their recovery plans to help grow revenue and re-shape the organization into a permanently leaner, simpler and more efficient model. Return to Work strategies are now in place to help leaders, managers and staff navigate through new realities in terms of managing customer interactions and team performance, where expectations and needs have shifted considerably.

Patrick McGillycuddy, Sales Director, Volkswagen Group UK

Patrick McGillycuddy is the sales director for Volkswagen Group UK, responsible for the sale of every VW car in the UK, through the management of the sales relationship between the parent company and factory in Wolfsburg, Germany and the franchisees, the length and breadth of the country.

In March 2019, nearly half a million cars were sold across the automotive sector during this annual peak trading month. However, in March 2020, as the pandemic hit and lockdown began, VWG, like all other manufacturers, were approaching the most important trading period of the year, linked to the new 2020 registration process. Across the industry, less than half the March 2019 number of cars were able to be sold.

Patrick described the timing as the worst possible, for the business and the industry alike. He went on to share, in light of this, how he led during this period, together with his personal insights and reflections.

Building dealer confidence, desire, seeing the opportunities rather than the problems

Patrick explained, with things moving so quickly, how he and his team worked tirelessly to support the dealerships, working shoulder to shoulder with them to protect the dealerships' costs and outlays as well as simplifying the working practices to make it easier for them to operate.

He went on to explain that having dealt with franchisees' early anxieties, it then became the challenge of, despite lockdown and so many dealership staff furloughed, helping them to unlock the large number of customers at various stages of the buying process. There was a sense in many areas that everything had ground to a halt, so he set out to build dealer confidence, desire and willingness to see the opportunities rather than the problems. Patrick stressed how he embarked upon a process of constant communication to help the dealerships understand what was happening, how VWG were responding, as well as the potential opportunities the virtual world now presented. He said in many ways it was getting them to think about what was possible rather than the problems. Rather than seeing the inability to do test drives, face-to-face selling and the whole dealership experience being curtailed, Patrick and his team encouraged them to think more broadly about virtual working utilizing existing product videos, informal virtual calls and virtual product launches, all designed to keep the customer engaged.

Reactivating the business while walking the investment tightrope

Soon after lockdown, Patrick and his team set about creating an emergence plan to prepare dealerships for a return to a new normal. This proved to be his greatest challenge: with dealerships locked down and most of their teams furloughed, franchisees were naturally focused on suppressing the cost base with no sign of revenue on the horizon. But this proved a conundrum: Patrick recognized the need to get teams back to create the new normal to ensure the dealerships were ready to go, but bringing them back incurred immediate expense.

Patrick explained how he was walking the investment tightrope – needing to bring people back to prepare the business v. incurred costs, and all while there was no sign of lockdown being lifted. That said, he was clear from conversations in the sector and prior governmental announcements that the time frame from announcement to delivery was becoming increasingly shorter as the UK government battled with containing the virus but also getting the economy moving.

Patrick embarked upon a process of influencing the franchisees by giving them confidence and belief that it was OK to trade, and engendering a momentum to act. He explained how he had to be tenacious and determined in constantly demonstrating the opportunities as he sought to release some from their lockdown mentality.

'Releasing the lockdown mentality'

Behind the scenes, Patrick and his team worked hard to push through changes that had long been desired, but had also been on the slow burn, overrun by the immediate challenges of the day. So, working with haste and focus with his colleagues in finance services and IT, they were able to deliver projects in a matter of weeks, including online finance as well as online contract hire, which all served to demonstrate the art of the possible and equally loosen the lockdown mindset.

Breaking the myths – collaboration

VWG UK is focused on five core brands – Volkswagen, Audi, Skoda, Seat and VW Commercial Vehicles – and although housed on the same site, collaboration had always been the exception rather than the rule. This wasn't because of any innate lack of desire or internal competition, but due to the fact that as a manufacturing and supply business, each brand operates from different factories, in different countries, with different priorities, strategies and focuses, which has the impact of driving the brands apart rather than encouraging collaboration.

The pandemic became a turning point, as Patrick explained that despite different pressures, priorities and plans, which cause each of the brands to see things through a different lens, when everything is pared back to the fundamental basics of business – the ability to generate revenue – there is a natural alignment. He further explained that 'when you focus on this at the simplest level, we have far more in common than we have differences, and this drove us together'. He shared that he and his fellow brand sales directors collaborated extensively to ensure a common approach, thinking and strategies with all the dealerships, so that they experienced common support, continuity and consistency, regardless of which brand they were or their location.

Patrick concluded that the pandemic had allowed a number of long-held business myths to be challenged:

- that the brands are so unique and different, there are too many differences to work together;
- that the different priorities, markets and focuses mean there is less need to collaborate;
- that the fundamental differences would mean that it would take too much time, effort and energy to collaborate.

Finally, Patrick stressed how the pace had been so relentless that he hadn't given himself time to stop and reflect. He explained that for many, the pandemic had been the opportunity to take stock, but for himself and his colleagues, the amount of activity had meant that only now, some three months on, was he reflecting back and learning. He was pleased with what had been achieved but recognized that it had been at the cost of considerable time, effort and energy. His team needed to pause to reflect upon what had been learned and most importantly, not lose the benefits of the new ways of working, he felt. He stressed that the period had challenged a lot of engrained thinking and he believed that they needed to capitalize upon this further going forward.

Gill Palfrey-Hill, Director of Global Talent & People Development, Specsavers

Gill Palfrey-Hill is now the UK Global Talent and OE Director, Costa Coffee, but at the time of the pandemic, she was Director of Global Talent & People Development for Specsavers, with responsibility for teams within the UK and matrix teams across the Specsavers globe, with businesses trading in the Netherlands, Norway, Sweden, Denmark, Finland, Spain, Australia and New Zealand. This highly specialized business is renowned for its optometry, audiology and healthcare services, through in excess of 2,000 stores, with 37,000 employees supporting over 1.4 million customers a week.

As the pandemic struck, the business continued to trade, providing support to customers with urgent healthcare requirements, while in the background all non-store staff moved to working remotely. With offices in Guernsey, Southampton, Nottingham and across the Nordics, Australia and New Zealand, remote working was not new. However, running the whole business virtually posed a fresh challenge.

During this period, Gill worked extensively with her peers and senior leadership team to provide the infrastructure to enable the stores to continue to operate and her teams to support this. Gill's experience and practical insights of leading her team through this are shared below.

Heightened engagement and support

Gill described how prior to the pandemic, the team had an informal Monday morning huddle to share priorities and focus for the ensuing week(s) ahead. With the onset of remote working, the huddle became a more formalized process, with a fixed virtual call, which provided the foundation for the team's engagement. Gill said that the huddle was quite informal and relaxed to kick off the week but she recognized that the virtual session, although equally relaxed, needed to meet more far-reaching aims of engagement, collaboration and support, keeping the team connected to each other. She explained further that rather than the informal conversations and unstructured nature of the huddle, this call provided the opportunity for every individual to share:

- their priorities for the week;
- their concerns, worries and what was on their mind;
- areas where they would welcome help and support.

Gill stressed that this process not only provided visibility to each team member with their respective priorities, but it also identified potential interdependencies and opportunities to collaborate. She also explained that at times, she would particularly seek out potential areas of collaboration, even if they weren't initially overt. She regarded this as essential for mutual peer support, learning and engagement, thereby ensuring individuals didn't become isolated and wholly consumed with their own priorities. This process furthermore enabled Gill to recognize where she should invest her efforts and shape her own week, particularly in terms of those individuals who were under the most pressure or were requiring the greatest amount of support.

In addition to regular 1:1 check-ins, Gill introduced a team midweek check-in as an informal catch-up, which was intended less as a business update on progress and more as an opportunity to talk about everything but work. This was either a mid-morning coffee session or an early evening catch-up with drinks, where all the week's events were discussed, from the UK government's daily briefings to events at home and amusing incidents from far and wide. This proved highly effective for team engagement but also provided opportunities for informal connecting to limit the impact of remote working.

Challenging virtual conversations

As the weeks passed, Gill and her team led the process of handling challenging virtual conversations across the business as significant numbers of staff were furloughed. She described how the team stepped up to handle what were potentially emotionally charged conversations, which they were very mindful of conducting with the same level of care, concern and connectivity as if they were in the room. Gill described how they'd all heightened their skill levels to convey messages and lead discussions with increased sensitivity and empathy, while doing so down the lens of a camera.

In fact, she herself had to handle those same conversations with members of her own team, which she described as personally tough but equally she felt that she'd handled these with the care and sensitivity they warranted. She went on to share that although these team members no longer attended the Monday call, all without exception joined every one of the ensuing mid-week check-ins, which she regarded as a sign of how well the whole process had been handled.

Finally, Gill reflected that this experience had encouraged her to invest even more time in her team. She had always been focused upon them and their success, but this period had intensified her focus on their needs and concerns. She stressed that working remotely had meant that she'd really tuned in, and listened even more acutely, to what was being said, as well as picking up the subtleties of the underlying cues that individuals weren't necessarily always willing to share spontaneously. Like never before, individuals' work and home lives merged, she reflected, and therefore the role of the leader was to really understand the whole person and their particular circumstances.

Anil Patel, Chief Executive Officer, Virtual Manager

Earlier, we learned about Anil Patel and his desire to obtain 'in the moment data' from afar. Driven by this, he and his business partner Neil Fillingham created the groundbreaking business Virtual Manager, a compliance-based software company, having met playing sport together in 2013.

Anil is chief executive officer of the business, which has offices in Brisbane, Australia and Rochester, New York, together with software engineers based in Melbourne and configuration teams in Manila in the Philippines and Stalingrad in Russia. The core business provides innovative software algorithms that enable businesses to identify and resolve issues from a distance, delegate and allocate tasks, and identify ineffectiveness in working practices, as well as potential areas of concern. This approach fundamentally addressed the major concern that faced him in Shell, with 300 sites: how to know how the business was performing at any moment from afar.

At the point of the coronavirus pandemic striking Australia, from March 2020, the business had a 70 per cent client base in the US, 20 per cent in Australia and 10 per cent in the UK. The core US business was built upon the recording, monitoring and scheduling of cleansing routines, replacing laborious paper and pen activities with simple iPad/iPhone touch points that registered data in real time, allowing virtual monitoring and scheduling. A typical US hospital contains circa 500 beds, with between 3 and 4km of workspace and therefore the Virtual Manager allowed supervisors to identify risks, monitor completed work and create schedules from a remote position.

With the Australian business built upon the hospitality, travel and entertainment industries, the business abruptly closed following the Australian government's rapid lockdown. How Anil and his team responded to the problems of the pandemic is described below.

Agility and adaptation

In contrast with Australia, the opportunities in the US business began to increase as hospital cleansing intensified and the demand for the Virtual Manager grew. However, this posed a number of major problems for Anil and his team:

- no site visits were allowed to install the software;
- no direct face-to-face, practical training to use Virtual Manager could be provided;
- fundamentally, there was no way of surveying the hospital to identify the pinch points and most appropriate locations for installing the data gathering elements for the Virtual Manager app.

With speed and agility, the business introduced remote training modules and made fundamental revisions to the existing product to enable it to be much easier to install remotely.

Instead of providing the normal, full installation, Anil and his team went from this to the very basic, simple but effective approach of cleaning staff positioning QR codes strategically around the sites. This had the impact of enabling live data to be gathered, calculated and fed into the data analytics in order to refine the algorithm and provide supervisors with the required decision-making information. Furthermore, in the past, the normal, full installation typically took four weeks. Instead, with cleaners despatched across a hospital, this labour-intensive version was achieved in two hours! An additional and major benefit from this work was that the hospital staff were able to track Covid-19 pressure points and contain outbreaks through analysing individual interactions and the range of contacts made, giving staff and visitors alike confidence to move freely in and out of the hospital.

Culture of innovation: '20 per cent of their working week is dedicated to ideas generation'

A cultural norm for the business is that every individual is encouraged to continuously come up with new ideas – in fact, 20 per cent of their working week is dedicated to ideas generation. Anil explained that his business has great teams and individuals who are continually looking to find solutions to everyday problems and have a culture of test and build.

As the pandemic gripped the world, this activity intensified with daily calls across the globe from individuals examining the emerging impact of the pandemic and considering what the business response could be. The level of testing intensified too as promising ideas were quickly sense-checked with clients before being trialled within 48 hours and decisions made about whether to progress or abandon almost immediately. This speed and agility meant that the business constantly sought to adapt and provide responses to potential needs highlighted through the pandemic.

Virtual working as an enabler rather than a barrier

Not surprisingly, the business has always been a virtual organization and a 24-hour operation. The internal data management and team alignment means that at any point, Anil can assess project progress from his office in Queensland as products commence development at the start of the working day in Australia before being passed on to Manila, Stalingrad and finally, the US. With this level of streamlining and integration, the business is able to optimize time zones rather than the time zones being a barrier to business practice. The team are also very well versed in having highly participative calls involving 20-plus team members contributing their ideas and thoughts.

Anil reflected that he believed the business's agility and innovation culture had enabled it to adapt quickly and seize the opportunities presented rather than the problems created by the pandemic. He commented that, fortunately, for 18 months prior he had particularly focused on bringing together the business, to share the same cultural values and increase alignment. Before this, he had experienced the business at times pulling in different directions due to its rapid growth. Every individual, from CEO to Helpdesk team, was involved and he believes this alignment and cohesiveness were critical to survival and enabled everyone to cope and pull together during the first and subsequent lockdown periods in 2020.

Anil also reflected that working remotely had become custom and practice before the pandemic. For some years, they had used tools such as Zoom and Slack before they became mainstream and therefore they were very fortunate to have already engrained this within the operation. Finally, when the crisis first hit and closed the Australian business in early 2020, Anil noticed other operations cutting back and reducing staff numbers, but on reflection he was pleased that he resisted the temptation to make redundancies and instead took the bold decision to recruit even more talented individuals, placing the business in an even stronger position going forward.

Jeremy Phillips-Powell, Group Talent Director, Rentokil Initial

Jeremy Phillips-Powell is the group talent director for FTSE 40 company Rentokil Initial, the world's largest pest control and hygiene business. It operates in over 80 countries through 43,000 employees and was named 'the best place to work' in 2019 by Indeed, as well as being recognized by *Management Today* in the same year for being Britain's most admired company for diversity and inclusion.

In our interview, Jeremy explained that this high-performing business had grown rapidly over the last five years through both market penetration and acquisition strategies. This growth has resulted in around two-thirds of the business, across the world, being focused upon pest control and being primarily based in and around major towns and cities with a large client base in the hotel, catering, restaurant and entertainment industries. He went on to explain that as the pandemic spread across the world and into its primary markets such as Asia, North America, Europe and the UK, the business faced the challenge of one of its key service lines predominantly servicing customers in sectors that had temporarily reduced trading. Jeremy shared both how Rentokil Initial responded to the challenges, as well as his own insights and learning below.

Pace and agility

In the first instance, Jeremy described how the business transformed and realigned its focus and priorities. Despite the growth in recent years of pest control, when the pandemic hit the hygiene business, with its cleaning and disinfecting services, was still one of the largest players in the world. Very quickly, the business pivoted towards providing hygiene and disinfection services that provided new revenue streams while other business lines were impacted. This required the deployment and hiring of 8,000 staff from across 60 countries to service new contracts, which meant once more the business had to operate with agility and pace in deploying teams to new locations as well as ramping up the local teams where needed.

Running focused and lean

Jeremy explained that as well as refocusing and pivoting the business in many countries, it also became a lot more focused. He reflected that, paradoxically, what he'd noticed pre-pandemic and became more transparent during the lockdown was that in most businesses:

- conscientious individuals tend to fill the time they have available during the day;
- equally, leaders tend to keep their teams busy and use any available capacity;
- if there's budget available, it tends to be used.

Jeremy went on to explain that when a significant event like the pandemic occurs, out of necessity you tend to focus on what really matters and with less budget available, it's amazing what can be achieved. He stressed that this wasn't just about cutting costs, but about being more clinical with what individuals and teams focused on and being prepared to say no to things more than yes, with the overriding question and principle of 'Will this move the business on and in simple terms, will this make the boat go faster?'

Communicating with a balance of realism and confidence

Jeremy explained how from the very start of the crisis the senior team communicated openly and transparently. He described how in every conversation, they were upfront with people, treating them like adults by sharing all the information and explaining not just how the business was doing, but how it was being affected here and now. He stressed that the approach shared the reality of the situation but also the reasons to be positive in terms of the foundations of the business and the actions being taken.

'People will take a lot of sh*t – but what they won't take is bullsh*t!'

Referencing the Napoleon quote – 'In a crisis the role of the leader is to define reality and give hope' – he went on to expand upon this by sharing, from his extensive experience during difficult times, 'People will take a lot of sh*t, but what they won't take is bullsh*t!' He emphasized how he'd seen people go beyond expectations because of the honesty and trust engendered by the leader.

Prepared to take the right actions, quickly and decisively

In many ways, this has been captured earlier though it has a particular resonance and significance in its own right and so has been also highlighted here in terms of the personal actions taken by the executive team. As the implications of the pandemic emerged and the impact and hardship it created for employees across the globe became apparent, senior leaders led the way, with management across the globe taking pay waivers as soon as the impact on the business became evident. Senior managers also donated all or parts of their salaries to an employee fund for colleagues around the world who were experiencing genuine hardship resulting from the pandemic.

Care, empathy and respect for how we treat people

Jeremy went on to explain that in a people-dependent and -rich business like Rentokil Initial, this pervaded all that they did. As in many businesses, significant numbers of employees across the globe were impacted by actions such as being placed on furlough, but that didn't stop the level of care and concern shown. In the UK, a bi-weekly newsletter tailored directly to the furloughed teams provided updates, information and guidance. Equally, the UK business through their links with the retail and distribution sectors were able to offer individuals the opportunity to use their skills outside of Rentokil for good causes and with other employers on a temporary basis.

As the easing of the first lockdown started to take place, the Rentokil HR team worked with IT to create an app that allowed individuals to reserve space in the office, enabling the facilities teams to manage capacity and ensure social distancing while also allowing Rentokil to trace the contacts of employees, should someone later develop Covid-19 symptoms. Once more, care, support and individual needs were placed at the centre of the decision-making.

Remote working is here to stay

Jeremy emphasized that a large proportion of the business operated in the field and working remotely from home was already in place some of the time for many employees. During the pandemic, as remote working increased exponentially, Rentokil Initial employees were able to easily adapt to and embrace this new way of working. An internal company survey of employees working remotely showed that:

- eighty-five per cent of the Rentokil Initial employees believe that the company has implemented effective remote working systems;
- eighty-two per cent feel part of a team despite working remotely;
- ninety per cent believe they have the resources to do their job effectively while working remotely;
- eighty-five per cent stated that working remotely had enabled them to work productively.

The employees were then asked to consider the statistics below pre/post the pandemic.

Pre-Covid: 55 per cent worked in a physical workspace (office, branch, warehouse);

Post-Covid: only 10 per cent wanted to return to a physical environment;

Pre-Covid: only 7 per cent worked remotely;

Post-Covid: 27 per cent wanted to work remotely exclusively;

Pre-Covid: 38 per cent worked in both physical and virtual workspaces;

Post-Covid: 63 per cent would like to continue with both the physical and virtual workplace.

Jeremy summarized this in quite simple terms: despite the preconceptions before Covid, virtual workspaces and remote working for RI is here to stay.

Going even more digital

Jeremy described this as 'if you weren't on the digital bus beforehand, you are now'. The onset of the pandemic saw the weekly uptake of online learning double from 30,000 to more than 60,000 individual sessions. This was supported by a range of virtual classroom sessions for groups of leaders on Leading Remote Teams, Managing Performance, Resilience and Well-being, and Financial Acumen. The digital transformation also resulted in over 19,000 e-letters being sent to employees over the three-month period of the first lockdown.

Finally, Jeremy reflected on how much had been learned not just about leaders and how they'd led the business, but also what constitutes leadership talent going forward. He went on to explain that the pandemic had revealed new types of leaders who had risen to the occasion and had handled complex and challenging problems highly effectively. He concluded that those individuals who maybe in the past might have tended to shy away from the limelight were beginning to realign the way the business views talent going forward.

Richard Walgate, Director, North Division, B&Q

Richard Walgate has worked in retail for over 30 years and is B&Q's Director, North Division. He has a portfolio of some 170 stores across eight regions spanning the South Midlands and Wales through Northern England and Scotland. When the pandemic struck and the first UK lockdown was instigated on 23 March 2020,

B&Q closed all 288 of its stores, relying solely on click and collect. Over the ensuing weeks, the business transformed its approach and gradually began re-opening stores from the middle of April.

Richard has a reputation for his commercial outlook and is renowned for successfully grasping and seizing opportunities. As a result, he led the transformation of the sales process across the northern stores, which he described during this intense period as being both tough and enjoyable. During that time, he and his colleagues worked tirelessly to re-engineer the business to create a Covid-safe environment. Together, they created groundbreaking changes, as well has having some fundamental realizations. The insights and learning of Richard and his colleagues are captured below.

Business agility and speed of action

Richard explained that the challenge of the pandemic had helped him, and others, realize how much more agile the business could be, and in fact had become, during the crisis. He stressed that 'we underestimated what could be achieved, at pace when under the extreme pressure of the pandemic'. The business became more agile in terms of debate, making decisions and achieving 'cut through'. He illustrated this by referring to B&Q's digital platforms and concluded that 'prior to the pandemic, we believed that we were very adept and at the forefront of digital. The pandemic proved we could push those boundaries even further. As a result, the level of action we've all taken means that we are not only digitally secure for now, but also for the future.'

Truly empowering teams with the freedom to act

Richard described how he and his colleagues had held the view that B&Q had an empowering work environment and this was true to a large degree. However, the pandemic really demonstrated what the true extent of this could be. In the past, leaders were often sent lengthy documents explaining what and how to operate. It didn't seem constraining but, on reflection, Richard recognized that in a drive for consistency, 'there were times that we may have been overly controlling, with very prescriptive explanations of what was required as a result. Communications have now been stripped back to basics'.

He went on to explain that with many staff furloughed and sales support office teams working remotely, the business had been run on a minimum structure. He then described how individuals and teams were truly stepping up and thriving from taking responsibility with freedom to act. No longer were there prescriptive documents, or directives on every issue. Instead, individuals are now trusted to act.

Pruning the decision-making tree

Richard explained that radical change started with the decision-making tree, which moved from the historical layers of decision hurdles to the clear appointment of a decision-maker. That individual was given the freedom to consult with whomever they needed to, in order to make the right call. He described how individuals stepped up and grew with this faster and more agile decentralized process.

Calling everything a priority: 'when it's about realigning the business in the turmoil of the pandemic, it's remarkable how quickly we can all make everything happen.'

Richard also had the realization that everyone tended to focus upon too many things and everything was traditionally called a priority. He went on to explain, 'It's been clear during the pandemic that it is impossible to have an enormous agenda. It has forced us to focus and as a result, we have achieved more.' He illustrated this with a systems integration and configuration example. Typically, a project of this nature would have been placed in the 'too difficult' box and delayed and pondered upon. However, 'when it's about realigning the business in the turmoil of the pandemic, it's remarkable how quickly we can all make everything happen.' What would have normally taken months, years or even been put off was achieved in a matter of weeks.

Leadership and collaboration

Richard was proud of how everyone had pulled together; the crisis had galvanized them all to work as one to re-engineer the business. He also spoke of how challenging it had been and the varying amounts of emotional support his team had needed. Once the stores started operating click and collect, he had daily calls with every one of his direct team, establishing not only what their plans were but also sharing successes and providing recognition.

He stressed, 'With so much happening, there was a danger we tend to focus on what we have to do rather than recognizing what we have done and our achievements, no matter how small' and he emphasized that everyone, in their own way, had achieved huge amounts. He concluded by reiterating the extent of the change that had been achieved in such a short time scale by challenging the norm of what was previously possible. In his view, the pandemic had increased the agility and collaboration across the business, which had resulted in phenomenal outcomes. He finished by stating all this had been achieved while the business was under intense scrutiny from the media and police alike, following the long trail of queues that emerged in the early days from the very loyal customer base who were content to wait in their cars for miles to collect their purchases. As ever, the integrity and professionalism of the business was maintained throughout. This was then followed by B&Q's socially distanced working practices, which set the benchmark for how other businesses were to trade effectively.

Penny Weatherup, Human Resources Director, Volkswagen Group UK

Penny Weatherup is the HR director for Volkswagen Group UK, which manages the prestigious brands of Volkswagen, Audi, Skoda, SEAT and VW Commercial Vehicles. With a franchise dealer network of 614 sites across the UK, Volkswagen Group UK accounts for one in every five cars sold in the UK.

Based from the UK headquarters in Milton Keynes, as the first lockdown was announced in March 2020, and with the exception of TPS Parts, VWGUK's parts' business, which was servicing emergency and key worker vehicles, all the remaining 1,000 staff began working from home. Penny explained that like many other businesses, with the exception of the field teams, everyone else was neither used to nor fully equipped for an extended period of working from home. She shared her insights and learning below.

Accelerating the pace of change

In the first instance, Penny described the incisive action to equip every staff member with the infrastructure to enable roles that had been wholly office-based to operate for an extended period smoothly from home. In many other businesses, remote working had become custom and practice, but this had never been the case with this long-established, leading automotive manufacturer. Once this was overcome, the business brought the same level of rigour and speed to focus upon the digital platform, enabling team members to operate effectively. Penny stressed that the experience had engendered a pace and energy to make change happen, which had not been seen before. She attributed this not to a lack of drive, but more to the number of competing priorities as well as being a very process-driven business. She explained that in many ways, 'the formality of these processes meant at times we can overcomplicate things'.

The 2020 pandemic had enabled a speed that had not been seen before, underpinned by what Penny described as a deep pride in the organization and a desire to overcome the challenges. She illustrated this with a number of examples: a project that had been presented to the board and had agreement for a 12-month implementation plan was re-presented with amendments, which meant it could be achieved in a matter of months. At its simplest level, within her own function, a process that would normally take two to three days to produce the detailed output was achieved in a matter of hours, with the necessary data to act rather than the normal in-depth analysis.

The speed of action also transcended to the way in which people were managed. When it became clear that the dealerships were unable to trade, the tough decision was made to furlough 45 per cent of Milton Keynes and field-based teams. All furloughed staff continued to be handled with care and sensitivity; in fact, within 24 hours of the decision being made, individuals had all received a personal 1:1 conversation.

Leadership capability

Penny went on to explain that she and her fellow board of management colleagues took the opportunity posed by the pandemic to take an even more rigorous review of the business priorities and as a result, accelerated the progress on a number of aspirational strategic topics. The speed and agility demonstrated by the business also highlighted the quality and depth of the leadership capability across the operation. There were numerous examples of leaders stepping up and thriving in the environment by taking the initiative and making significant change happen. She further shared that it had also exposed those who were less capable of leading during the period of great ambiguity and uncertainty created by the pandemic.

New ways of working: 'Speak Up' barometer

As Penny explained earlier, at the outset, working remotely was not an engrained practice within the business. There were field teams working closely with the network, but the majority of the Volkswagen Group team were based at its site in Milton Keynes. During this period, Penny launched their 'Speak Up' barometer to gauge how effectively the process was being handled. The results indicated high levels of satisfaction with both how the business was communicating and managing the process, as well as the ability to work remotely. Increased flexibility had been highly valued by the teams, though much clearly rested on individuals' own ability to manage themselves and their priorities.

Penny went on to explain that the business did tend to have a meetings culture and that had continued during the lockdown. It was clear from the results that these had become more focused and productive, though she felt there was a danger of Skype fatigue. Penny also shared that she was aware of significant amounts of 'day creep'. With everyone available at home, the early disciplines of limiting the working day had started to become eroded. With earlier starts and later meetings entering individuals' diaries, she had become very conscious of how the new normal was evolving.

As we concluded our discussions, Penny reflected on how far the business had come during the pandemic and the satisfaction with what had been achieved. She was equally mindful that although the new ways of working had been thrust upon everyone, it had proved so successful that these needed to be harnessed going forward; a return to the old ways was not an option.

Axel Zeltner, Director, Deloitte Deutschland

Axel Zeltner is a director in Deloitte Deutschland based in Munich and he shared his experiences of leading through the coronavirus pandemic. He began by contextualizing the situation in Germany, which had introduced restrictions on gatherings, social distancing and the closure of schools in early March 2020 – sooner than the UK started to introduce restrictions – and formally entered lockdown on 20 March. As a result, by the middle of April 2020, the German government had begun to ease lockdown and by the middle of June, offices were opened under strict social distancing guidelines.

Axel clarified that although the government provided guidance, the decisions on how this was actually implemented were determined by the 15 individual states of Germany – a process very much like the US system of government policy and state decision-making. He went on to explain that some of the decisions and differences were quite far-reaching – for example, Southern Bavaria and Baden-Württemberg, which had historically always been more cautious and conservative in their approaches, adopted a rigid lockdown, while Mecklenburg,

Berlin and Lower Saxony applied a more relaxed approach – for example, most stores were open and groups of up to 50 could meet together. This resulted in individuals taking advantage of the various differences, such as readily travelling across states to access opportunities denied in their own areas. The diversity in decision-making also had the impact of determining who could go to the beach and who couldn't, as some states stipulated that travelling to the beaches, i.e. the Northern Baltic Islands, was prohibited, while others encouraged it. Axel explained that in some ways the decisions were a reflection of the infection rate, however, these differences also reflected long-held different philosophical positions.

Formalize the informal

Axel explained that prior to the pandemic, he would spend 75 per cent of his time working from the Munich office, servicing clients as well as providing support to his team of 11. Typically, like other leaders, he would have numerous informal conversations as he would be on hand to support and guide his teams. As the pandemic struck and all the team moved to remote working, he began to formalize the informal.

To compensate for the lack of these informal catch-ups, Axel scheduled bi-weekly sessions with each of his team members. The purpose of these was to understand how they were coping and progressing with their work, as well as finding out how they were and to understand more about their lives and families.

'Everything but work'

Axel complemented these sessions with a virtual beer, whereby the whole team came together on a Thursday to share everything but work. He also instigated a weekly business call, which was designed to share business updates but also to provide a vehicle for team members to share concerns, thoughts and ideas. As the initial lockdown eased and team members began to return to the office on a rotating basis, he continued with the established practice of virtual calls as the only constant way of working and also provided the routine that team members could work around.

Virtual conferences for networking

Axel explained that conferences were part of the Deloitte Deutschland infrastructure that encouraged cross-fertilization of ideas and networking. The traditional June conference, which enables 150 partners, directors and team members to come together, still took place virtually and despite some scepticism as to how the networking element would be achieved, this proved highly productive. Much thought had been given to allow team members to join three breakout sessions, each with small groups requiring some preparation so that all could gain and contribute, regardless of the hierarchy.

Finally, Axel reflected how he'd become more efficient and organized as the weeks progressed, recognizing the draining impact of days full of Zoom calls. He introduced formal breaks between calls, so reducing the intensity of the day and helping to increase the quality of his contribution. He also said he'd become more challenging in his own mind around whether he really needed a face-to-face meeting or not and whether a virtual call would be equally effective and therefore a more productive use of his time. For Axel, his experiences in the early months of the pandemic had given him new levels of self-discipline and focus, as well increasing the engagement of his team even further.

Leading remote teams during the coronavirus pandemic: a summary

From our conversations with these insightful leaders, as well as our work with hundreds of leaders in the UK, Europe, Asia, the Middle East and Pacific regions through our virtual leadership learning sessions, we have been able to summarize the learning and core components of leading teams through the pandemic with the following model:

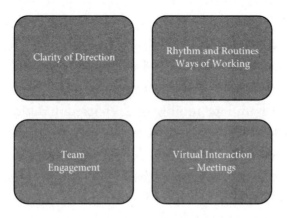

Clarity of direction

As with any team, clarity of direction in terms of where the team is heading and what it's seeking to achieve is fundamental to success. In leading remote teams through the pandemic, it has been of paramount importance in providing individuals and the wider team with the context to make their own decisions.

The 2020 pandemic has created a level of activity and intensity for individuals working in isolation that has never been experienced before. What we have learned is that individuals can become so absorbed in the *doing* that they lose sight of the priorities and above all, the core purpose of their role. We have seen leaders continually providing clarity of where the team is heading as well as progress towards this as a means of supporting team members' understanding of not just the context but also their own contribution to success.

In working in isolation, it has become very apparent that individuals have often become detached from the wider picture and so absorbed in their own world that their view of reality can often be distorted. They don't have those around them in the normal workplace who can share different perspectives and realign thinking. Clarity of direction in both the physical and virtual world is thus embodied in individual objectives/targets and the explicit link of these to the business priorities and aspirations. The most successful leaders provided this clarity in ways that engendered commitment and ownership, as well as a level of understanding that enabled individuals to take appropriate decisions for themselves, without regular guidance.

In the early stages of the pandemic, we saw businesses narrow their focus and streamline their operations, which resulted in individuals and teams reducing the number of priorities and being able to focus and have real clarity of direction. The pandemic has forced individuals and teams to establish what really was achievable together with what really mattered and ensured the business focused on this and this alone, rather than wider-ranging priorities that dilute focus and energy.

Leaders who have never previously managed from afar have been focused into so doing from behind a computer screen. Many have struggled with this, not because they lack the fundamental skills, but because have found it so unfamiliar and unnatural not to be face to face and physically together. Many have spoken about the difficulties of reading body language and the normal clues that they would readily spot in a physical environment. That said, our work has shown that the skills in the virtual world are fundamentally the same, though some such as observation and listening have to be even more highly tuned. I liken this very much to the days when a phone call was literally listening and talking, and phones didn't have a camera image. On these occasions, the quality of our listening tended to intensify as we could hear every sigh, every doubt and every last word. In many ways our senses became heightened and this applies too in the virtual world, where individuals at the other end of a lens may be more stilted and less natural, but this is just the process of leaders adjusting their senses to the new normal.

One particular aspect that has proved challenging for many leaders in the context of the above is the managing of performance. In examining this further, it is worth exploring the four key components of how performance is assessed.

1) Role purpose

    This is a clear, succinct statement of why the role exists and is essential in both the physical and the virtual world. This provides both the leader and team member with real clarity of focus.

    Role purpose is not a job title or a list of responsibilities but a no-nonsense, 'non-management-speak' clear statement of why the role exists.

    For example:

        People Partner: 'ensuring we have the right people with the right skills for both now and in the future'
        Rather than: 'supporting, guiding and advising managers on people issues'

The former statement provides clarity of direction and purpose, while the latter statement describes some of the activities involved.

Supply chain leader: 'ensure every store has the right products in the right location at the right time'

Rather than: 'managing the supply chain and business infrastructure to meet our objectives'

2) Objectives

Stick to five or six key objectives rather than a plethora of competing objectives that confuse and dilute success, which once more is equally important in both the physical and virtual world.

3) Quantitative measures

These are the metrics such as sales, profit, margin, growth, cost engagement, service and customer satisfaction. Again, these should be the same in both the physical and virtual world and typically depicted in business performance dashboards or scorecards. They demonstrate what has been achieved and the outcomes of actions.

However, the major difference in the managing of performance concerns the fourth component, qualitative measures.

4) Qualitative measures

These are the measures that depict how things have been done, typically gained through observation or feedback from others. This has proven to be particularly difficult in the virtual world but not impossible, and has required leaders to:

- Become even more inquisitive and curious in their discussions with team members to really build a picture of how the individual has approached or handled a particular task. By listening attentively to their responses and their descriptions, the leader can build a rich picture of the 'what' and most importantly the 'how' actions have taken place, which enables the leader to contrast with their own thinking. In many ways, this should be no different to the normal physical workplace, however with leaders' own first-hand observations, they are often too hasty to jump to conclusions and intervene rather than understanding an individual's thinking.

- Obtain insights and observations from colleagues who may have had first-hand dealings with team members. Equally, team members themselves often have insights on their own colleagues from collaborative working, and discreet unobtrusive questions can elicit a wealth of behavioural data.

Finally, even in the virtual world, there are opportunities to join team members during virtual interactions with customers and colleagues.

Rhythm and routines: ways of working

The pandemic has thrust remote working upon a population across the globe who had never previously worked from home and the establishment of new rhythms and routines has been essential to provide structure and support to the working week for all. This period has also resulted in many businesses challenging established ways of working. As highlighted by many leaders in this chapter, businesses have become more agile and streamlined through the flushing out of unnecessary and stagnant practices that have never previously been questioned. This has resulted in the swathes of reports, spreadsheets and internal hurdles that have traditionally slowed decision-making being removed, allowing quicker decisions to be made. For many, the crisis of the pandemic has established new norms and a focus on speed rather than perfection, as businesses have innovated and shaken up their thinking. Underpinning these changes, leaders have introduced new working practices to cement the teams' ways of operating:

Team meetings

In the early stages of the pandemic, leaders tended to provide daily updates and make quick decisions. As businesses stabilized, the rhythm and routines became weekly meetings at fixed times to enable team members to build this into their schedules.

From our work, we are also aware that meetings have become more focused, with leaders being clear on the purpose, which is one or more of the following:

a) share information;
b) generate ideas;
c) make decisions.

In reality, this shouldn't be any different from pre-pandemic. That said, from our experience, too many businesses had lapsed into a meetings culture of attendance and presenteeism without due regard to their role, the real purpose and desired outcomes.

Leaders also introduced informal team meetings during the week, with a coffee call or after-work drink to have informal chats and catch-ups. These proved to be highly productive for maintaining relationships and enhancing engagement, as well as informally providing leaders with insights into the individuals' mindsets, concerns and broader pressures.

Individual meetings

Leaders spoke about how important it was to schedule these, too, to provide more routine to team members' working weeks, for checking in, catching up and supporting them in the challenges they were facing.

It has become apparent that working remotely, for many team members, has been challenging in terms of:

- right environment – working from home has meant individuals balancing the challenges of educating their children, keeping them occupied, supporting other family members, competing for Wi-Fi access as well as trying to do their job, all in the same work/ home space, while some others, who live alone, have found the relentless solitude both demanding and draining;
- ability to manage themselves – working remotely has required heightened levels of self-discipline to focus, prioritize and self-motivate. Some individuals have thrived in this environment, others have needed more support to learn to manage themselves. We know from our own in-company research, from hundreds of leaders in Australia, New Zealand, throughout Asia, Europe, Latin America and the Middle East from our Virtual Leadership Workshops throughout 2020, that individuals have relished the flexibility offered by home working and that has been reflected in generally higher productivity. That said, though many individuals have spoken of increased productivity, a significant number have attributed this not to more efficient practices, but more to working longer hours; with journey times saved, the working day has lengthened. The effect of no journey time, though convenient, has also had the impact of reducing the opportunity to allow time to 'tune into work' from the journey in and 'tune out of work' on the journey home;
- technology – with so many working from home, the local pressures on bandwidth as well as the in-home battles for Wi-Fi, together with the ability to access the businesses' own systems, which have never been designed for remote working, also contributed to intensifying pressures and challenges;

- managing work/life balance. This was a test for many pre-pandemic and on the face of it might seem resolved with no travel time and being permanently in the home environment. However, this posed new challenges, with individuals actually working longer days, as well as work and life merging as one. In fact, in some ways, individuals are no longer working at home, but living at work as the boundaries of work and life blur into one. As the weeks passed, we became more aware that meetings were being organized both earlier and later in the day – the working day was lengthening and many were becoming fatigued by the endless days in front of a screen.

Collaboration between departments

It was evident that when there was an explicit and overt need for individuals from different departments to jointly work on issues, these became scheduled into the rhythm and routines of the week. However, remote working seems to have stifled the informal opportunities to collaborate.

In the normal office environment, leaders would bump into colleagues from other functions while grabbing a coffee or walking the floor. This informal event would often reveal relevant insights and areas of potential mutual interest, which weren't otherwise necessarily obvious and therefore wouldn't necessitate a formal calendar invite.

In effect, though working from home has proved productive, it has effectively prevented this informal contact and therefore many leaders have built into their schedules informal calls with colleagues to have a coffee and share perspectives, rather than only coming together for a specific task purpose.

The disciplined, working from home with a clear purpose to meetings approach, though bringing more efficiency has resulted in a reluctance to meet for informal purposes, thereby increasing the number of missed opportunities to collaborate between departments, which naturally occurs in a physical environment.

Many leaders have begun to rejuvenate their networks, connecting with those who they may not have had explicit business needs to work together with, but were part of their network pre-pandemic. In reconnecting, many have benefitted from the sharing of insights and learning from other parts of the business, which for many has acted as a stimulus for new thinking. This has resulted in a number of new, improved ways of working and, in more than one instance, identification of significant commercial opportunities.

Team engagement

The fundamental skill for leading remotely, as you will have read throughout Chapter 2, is the leader's ability to encourage individuals and teams to take ownership and responsibility and be able to be self-standing. This has become even more apparent during the pandemic. As we described in Chapter 1, the reason so many leaders failed in progressing from a single site to a multi-site leadership role was their inability to let go and empower others. This challenge intensified with individuals working from home, rendering leaders unable to consistently check, monitor, even listen in or wander over as they might in a workplace. Engagement, empowerment and ownership have become fundamental to success.

Individual engagement

During the pandemic, we saw leaders make a far more concerted effort to connect with their team themselves through both their formal check-ins as well as utilizing various chat forums such as WhatsApp, Yammer and WeChat.

What has been apparent is that individuals working in isolation can lose sight of what is being achieved. Equally, the remote working practice has at times seemed to induce distorted perspectives and therefore leaders have not only provided regular business updates but have also sought to stand back, reflect and share what has been achieved and connect individuals' contributions to overall success.

Greater collaboration

The solitary and isolating working practices of operating at home resulted in many leaders striving to encourage collaboration between team members as a way of increasing engagement. This was achieved through a variety of techniques:

- individuals took responsibility for projects on behalf of the team, resulting in a necessity to liaise and discuss with colleagues on a regular basis;
- pairs of team members were given the same objectives to encourage joint working on particular projects;
- individuals alternating in leading part of the entire team meeting;
- team meetings being used to update others about their respective work, resulting in team members identifying areas of mutual interest and collaboration;
- team members providing insights into what they had learned that week, rather than purely what they had done;
- team members being encouraged to reconnect with the network they had established in the physical world with a view to bringing thoughts, ideas and learning back to their team.

In all instances, leaders sought to encourage greater team interactivity rather than relying on just themselves as the sole source of individual and team engagement.

Walking the virtual floor

In the normal working environment, leaders would often walk the floor, choosing moments to have passing conversations with team members and colleagues alike. Though more challenging in the virtual world, it proved not beyond achievement. In fact, as Mike Hawes highlighted (see page 145), walking the floor virtually is essential for all leaders. This doesn't mean scheduling formal meetings but the more informal and spontaneous messaging through chat forums to see if it's convenient to have a quick chat or check-in. Clearly in the workplace, leaders would be able to see if it's a good moment to talk or not. In the virtual world, leaders have to rely on individuals managing that response and indicating the suitability to catch up. Obviously, the process is more stilted when remote, but nevertheless it has become part of the rhythm and routines of most leaders.

Return of furloughed team members

As the months progressed, teams started to evolve as furloughed team members began to return and became integrated back into the remote workplace. This has posed fresh challenges for leaders and furloughed members alike, with so many having been out of the new routines of the working environment for so long and having to adjust to new business priorities and ways of working and providing fresh integration challenges.

In fact, many leaders underestimated the impact of furlough on the individuals themselves. They may have misguidedly believed that it was very much like a team member returning from an extended holiday, rather than recognizing the need for re-orientation and realignment back to work. It has also been important to help team members manage their anxiety, concerns, confidence and attachment to the old ways of working.

Virtual interactions – the meetings

The final component of leading remote teams during the pandemic focuses upon how leaders actively conducted the meetings themselves, whether as a team or on a 1:1 basis.

As previously shared, the interactions themselves tended to have a far greater clarity of purpose:

- to share information;
- to generate ideas;
- to make decisions.

We are also aware that in addition to the ground rules/charter, which included cameras on, no distractions by browsing emails or searching other content, and expectations of collaboration and involvement, group sizes in some businesses were reduced.

Group sizes

In the early stages of the pandemic and working virtually down a lens, it has been easy for all and sundry to join, listen and contribute but for many leaders, this has proved impractical for making decisions.

As a result, and as highlighted by Debbie Edwards at Gap (see page 137), many have reduced the group size to those who need to be there to make a particular decision. Attendees were selected not based on hierarchy, but insight and relevant knowledge.

Understand team members, mindsets and perspectives

Throughout the coronavirus pandemic, like no other time, leaders had to continually listen, explore and seek to understand team members' mindsets and perspectives. This might sound illogical in that this should be the case in the normal physical world, however, as explained previously, the isolation clearly affected individuals in different ways as each grappled with their own work/home challenges. As many leaders have shared, though the skill requirements were essentially the same, the tensions and pressures of individuals working in the virtual world meant that the level of attentiveness had to be greater. That attentiveness was to understand their world, mindset and perspectives in order to help them manage things for themselves.

To encourage everyone to contribute, some leaders described adopting a structured approach with each individual sharing what was on their mind, their key learning and insights over the last week. This served not only to update colleagues but also provided the leader with insights into the pressures each person was facing. As previously mentioned, leaders often then encouraged team members to lead different parts of the meeting and to not always rely on the usual suspects to do so.

The encouraging of interactions also extended to more innovative ways of ensuring that meetings were stimulating. In addition to more conventional breakout groups, individuals leading elements and the introduction of fun activities such as quizzes and drink/chat sessions, leaders adopted even more engaging techniques, as time has progressed. These have included videos of team members' children reading out the latest business results in their own unique childlike ways along with images of famous personalities dubbed with narrative from leaders and individuals joining meetings with items from around their homes as a vehicle to share their thinking in a memorable way. All of these were designed to increase fun and engagement through the lengthening periods of isolation.

The coronavirus pandemic has, without doubt, tested and challenged leaders and individuals alike to adapt to the new normal and as the pandemic has continued, to be able to continually keep individuals and teams engaged and energized despite the restrictions on movement and connectivity.

CHAPTER SIX

Conclusions and Reflections

This book started by describing the challenges of stepping up from a single-site leadership role to a multi-site leadership role and the need to understand why so many leaders failed in so doing. Through that research, we were able to identify what really differentiated the outstanding from the average from the poor remote leader.

Over the years, multi-site leadership has grown to leading countries, regions, continents and globally. Throughout our research, the differentiated behaviours have been reinforced despite the growing magnitude of leaders' roles. The wealth of examples from the highly respected leaders is testament to that. However, throughout this research, leading remotely has tended to be associated with working on different sites or locations rather than working from home. There were clearly occasions in the past when this was the case – in fact, I first did so over 30 years ago. However, never has there been such a large proportion of many businesses' whole workforce being led from home as has occurred during the pandemic.

The pandemic intensified the need to work remotely. What became the skill set of some leaders became a necessary skill for most leaders as they sought to adapt to leading their teams in socially distanced workplaces or from home. This period has seen leaders making breakthroughs in the way in which their teams and businesses have operated and as we have learned in this book, a whole raft of changes:

- long-held traditional working practices have been shaken up for the better;
- businesses have become more agile, streamlined and effective;
- businesses have begun to really question what they stand for and what is important;
- internal problems and hurdles that slow progress have been stripped out;
- engrained thinking has been challenged – for example, the realization that home working can be highly productive, as demonstrated by numerous research studies;
- better use of the working day, with less time wasted travelling to and from locations;
- individuals have thrived from the freedom to manage their own days;
- above all, this new way of working has been underpinned by a real care and concern for others, which has been continually demonstrated by leaders.

We started by sharing the extensive research backed by the fantastic insights of leaders across the globe. The book then became overtaken by a new form of leading remotely, driven by the coronavirus pandemic. As we draw to a close, it's hard not to forget the impact of the pandemic with the intense and tragic loss of life, the number of businesses that have succumbed to bankruptcy, the vast swathes of job losses, the huge levels of debt and how all this has affected everyone both at the height of the crisis and as we move forward. That said, as highlighted above, businesses have been forced to change and there have been numerous related benefits. As we move to a more settled – albeit changed – way of working, the future will never be the same and that should be viewed as positive. That said, there are increasing signs that some businesses and leaders may not have learned from the experience, as I'm already seeing:

- individuals are starting to introduce more layers of structure;
- processes that slowed decision-making are gradually being reintroduced;
- the frantic pace of change that was instigated in the crisis stage is being sought to be maintained, creating fatigue among much of the workforce;
- in the now more settled period, there are attempts to close down the options of working flexibly and remotely, instead returning workforces to sites, while failing to take account of how individual mindsets have changed so much during the pandemic and the fact that many are already regarding flexible ways of working as being paramount in their future career decisions.

All of this raises the inevitable question: how does the research on leading remotely prior to the emergence of the pandemic compare with that during the pandemic? The answer is reasonably simple: although the context has changed, the challenges and pressures have intensified and leaders and team members themselves have become even more isolated, creating greater personal pressures, the skills and behaviours have proved to be consistent. Those leaders who had created dependency upon themselves, restricted the level of empowerment of their teams and weren't able to let go struggled along with their teams to adapt to working remotely. Fundamentally, whether pre- or post-pandemic, leaders and their teams need real clarity of direction about where the function is heading and their role within that, in order for individuals themselves to take ownership and responsibility, do their own thinking and make their own decisions.

The role of the remote leader is to help people to succeed for themselves in the context of the business priorities. This means having to really diagnose, enquire and listen in order to understand their team members' mindset, thoughts and perspectives on particular issues – in effect how they are looking at a situation in order to find the right ways forward for them using coaching and collaborating skills. That said, although the skills and behaviours are consistent, we did see an increasing level of explicit empathy, understanding and real concern for people demonstrated by leaders across the globe during the pandemic.

Throughout our global leadership sessions, we have heard from team members commenting on how much care and concern they have personally experienced. How leaders have truly become interested them and their lives, a behaviour that many would argue should have been prevalent before and may have been instinctive for some, but not the many.

Finally, despite the traumas of the pandemic, it has resulted in more versatile and capable leaders as the skill of leading remotely, previously the domain of the few, has become essential for all leaders.

Sources

Wright, Oliver and Laurence, Jeremy, 'NHS Darkest Day: Five More Hospitals Under Investigation for Neglect as Report Blames "Failings at Every Level" for 1,200 Deaths at Staffordshire Hospital', *Independent*, February 2013

'Mid Staffs NHS Trust Face Criminal Charges', *Guardian*, October 2015

Hutcheon, Paul, 'Scottish Government to Quit Crime Stats', *Herald*, June 2015

Yan, Holly, and Blackwell, Victor, 'Atlanta Police Defend Using Traffic Tickets to Fund Pay Increases', *CNN*, 2013

Kerr-Dineen, Luke, 'FIFA World Rankings a Joke', Schwartz, *USA Today*, 2015

Tweedale, Alistair, 'Belgium at No 1 After They Beat Israel, Despite Playing One Tournament in 13 Years', *Daily Telegraph*, October 2015

Peachey, Paul, 'Fiddled crime figures lead to under-reporting of rapes and other serious offences says report', *Independent*, April 2014

Lawson, Max; Parvez Butt, Anam; Harvey, Rowan; Sarosi, Diana; Coffey, Clare; Piaget, Kim; Thekkudan, Julie, 'Unpaid and Underpaid Care Work and the Global Inequality Crisis', Oxfam International, 20 January 2020. Available at: oxfam.org/en/research/time-care (accessed 10 December 2020)

Index

Note: page numbers in **bold** refer to diagrams, page numbers in *italics* refer to information contained in tables.